PRAISE FOR

"That's Just the Way Life Is..."

"...a fine piece of writing, honest, unflinching,...impressive work."

Peter Gibb
author of King OF Doubt, a memoir,
Teacher, Lecturer on memoir writing and mindfulness.

"This is a book not everyone will want to read...but everyone should... profound and moving, wonderfully well written."

Olivia Taylor-Young
FORMER Public Relations Director / Hospice Public Information Officer, San Jose, CA
retired newspaper / magazine columnist, U of Oregon Osher LifeLong Learning Institute

"It is well written, a very honest telling of your experience with your father's dying. The questions at the end are ...helpful and should generate valuable reflection."

Fred Grewe
Clergyman, Hospice at Providence Medical Facility, Medford, Oregon

BOOKS BY LESLIE COMPTON

**Dearest Minnie,
A Sailor's Story**
True Story, Teddy Roosevelt's Great White Fleet

That's Just the Way Life Is...
A Memoir

LESLIE COMPTON

THAT'S JUST THE WAY LIFE IS···
A MEMOIR

That's Just The Way Life Is
by Leslie Compton

Copyright ©2018 Leslie Compton
All rights reserved.

First Edition ©2018

FSP
FIRST STEPS
PUBLISHING

Published by
First Steps Publishing
PO Box 571
Gleneden Beach, Oregon 97388-0571
FirstStepsPublishing.com

This book is memoir. It reflects the author's present recollections of experiences over time. Some names and identifying details have been changed, ome events have been compressed, and some dialogue has been recreated to protect the privacy of the people involved.

No part of this publication may be reproduced or transmitted in any form or by any means, electronic or mechanical, without permission in writing from the publisher or author.

Poetry used within this book are from the author's mother's college collection of her favorite poems; to the publisher's knowledge, such works are free of known restrictions under copyright law, including all related and neighboring rights.

Library of Congress Control Number: 2018954445
Genre: memoir, death & dying

Cover Design by Suzanne Fyhrie Parrott
Cover photo *"Farmer in tractor preparing land with seedbed cultivator, sunset shot"*
©Valentin Valkov/Shutterstock.com
Cover images, *orange grove trees*, ©arka38/Shutterstock.com
Photo of Leslie Compton by William G. Compton © 2016

ISBN: 978-1-937333-71-3 (pbk)
ISBN: 978-1-937333-73-7 (hbk)
ISBN: 978-1-937333-72-0 (ebk)

10 9 8 7 6 5 4 3 2 1

Printed in the United States

For my father

CONTENTS

Praise for *That's Just the Way Life Is*............... 1
Books by Leslie Compton 2
That's Just the Way Life Is! 9
    January, 2000........................ 10
    February 33
    March................................ 91
    April................................ 169
    May.................................. 237
    Epilogue............................. 241
    Afterword 249
Thank you................................ 250
Note from the Author...................... 251
Discussion Questions 252

That's Just The Way Life Is

Grief is a journey, not a destination, and there is no one right way to travel, no shortcuts, no freeway. There are no five easy steps to pain free grieving. In *Winter Grief, Summer Grace*, James Miller said, 'The right way to grieve is *your* way. No one else in the world no matter how close they are has had your relationship with the person who has died. No one else has your temperament, or your unique ways of dealing with stress, or your previous experience with losses. No one else is you. So, the best way to move through this time of grief is your own way.'

(*When Your Parent Dies*, by Ron Klug, p.20)

Leslie Compton
June, 2018

That's Just the Way Life Is!

Memory

These are the joys that longest stay:
Little games we used to play;
Little bits of merry speech
Pedagogues can never teach:
What was loved and what despised,
What was scorned and what was prized;
Thoughts we scarcely dwelt upon
Till the friend of old had gone.

Strange how memory retains
Little of the larger gains
And so very firmly clings
To the tender, trivial things.
How he dressed and how he broke
Into laughter at a joke.
These when death has closed them all
Are the splendors we recall.

After time has soothed the pain
And we dare to talk again,
We remember, you and I,
Just the twinkle in the eye;
Just the coat upon the chair
Tossed so carelessly out there;
Unimportant once, and yet
These we never quite forget.

—Edgar A. Guest
*(From Mother's college collection
of her favorite poems)*

January, 2000

It's a frigid January day in Massachusetts with temperatures dropping into the teens, but our home is warm, inviting, enveloping me like a comfortable cocoon. My husband and I returned yesterday after spending the holidays with my widowed father in Northern California, making sure he had a good housekeeper and adequate resources to make his life easier. We then flew to Colorado to help our youngest son get through a financial crisis. I helped him create a budget with a ledger sheet to better manage his monthly income. He's in the army now, something he wanted to do after high school. He had had a long history of being unsettled. "I need some structure in my life," he told us. "The army will make sure that happens." After boot camp, he was transferred to Colorado Springs.

"You know, Jason, we can't do this again," my husband and I both stressed to him before we left. "You have to get your act together, and soon."

Family duties finally accomplished, holidays over, I have decided to set aside this entire day to spend in my loft surrounded by the panoramic view of newly fallen snow glistening in the bright sunlight. For the rest of this week, while Joe is at work, I plan to organize this area to become my sewing room, creating a healing and peaceful environment. I need this quiet time to recuperate from our trip and to settle myself after another corporate move.

The day is all mine. CDs are spinning on my portable boom box. Slow, melodic harmonies of violins, flutes, and guitars resonate throughout the room. I spend time sorting through numerous boxes of silk fabrics and lay out coordinating colors on my cutting table. The red silk ties I use for crazy quilts go into a new plastic bin, the blues and yellows in yet another. I separate the many trims into smaller containers, one for yarn, one for braid, and one for ribbon. The CD changer makes a clunky sound as the next selection is brought into play. Enya begins singing in her low, soft, sexy voice; a peaceful sound against the background of a grand piano.

The startling blare of a telephone from the floor below cuts through my semi-meditative calm. *Damn! Why am I always interrupted every time I carve out some time for myself?* I grudgingly race down the stairs to grab the receiver before the answering machine picks it up. But I know. Before I answer, I instinctively know. It's time. My knees begin to buckle, my throat tightens, and my heart starts to gallop at marathon speed. I wish I could avoid this whole moment, perhaps this entire next year. I manage to retrieve the intruding instrument from its cradle before the end of the third ring.

"Hello," I say, in what I hope sounds like an upbeat voice.

"Yaaaaah—it's Dad." He never calls me during the week, only on Sunday nights when the rates are cheaper. The time has come. That dreaded moment, the 'monkey' on Dad's back, as he always calls it, has finally revealed its ugly face. "My PSA results came back today, the nurse just called. It jumped from 125 to 800." A long, deafening silence follows while we both grasp the news. "I have an appointment with my urologist on Friday morning, so I will find out more at that time. Meanwhile, I am told to go to the hospital today for a bone scan."

"Oh, God, I am so sorry, Dad." Tears sting my eyes and roll down my face while I try to maintain some control in my voice. "You know I'll be there for you, I told you that just a couple of weeks ago. I'll be there in time for that doctor's visit. I'll pack a bag, make the reservations, and call you right back. I'll be there as soon as I can."

"I knew you would come." Then silence.

I don't know how long I have stood here holding what has become an ugly, loathsome, piece of black plastic in my hand. But I am quickly brought back to reality by the hideous monster screaming its bleep, bleep, bleep to let me know Daddy had disconnected.

How am I going to do this? How am I going to survive this ordeal? I am not, and never have been a good caregiver. When my boys were sick, I hastily put the aptly named plastic "throw-up bowl" next to their bed and retreated. That's how I care for sick people. I tried nursing school, but after only nine months I snatched my nursing cap off my head, threw it on the floor, and ran out of the hospital. Caring for the sick is definitely not my thing, but I will be there for him. To get through this moment, I begin to repeat over and over, *be in the 'now,' Leslie, don't think of what may come tomorrow.* Turning off my sewing machine, my CD player, and the lights in my loft, I mechanically make the necessary phone calls to again arrange for a flight across country, notify my husband, and repack my suitcase.

* * *

Twenty-four hours have elapsed since Dad made that life-changing phone call. I am flying at 35,000 feet through dense cloud cover and vicious storms. It's Thursday, January 19th. I have chosen the cheapest fare, a $99 special to Oakland, California, knowing I will probably make several cross-country trips in the next few months. There are two stopovers along the way; so, with the ride to and from both airports, it will take me fourteen hours to travel from coast to coast. I order a glass of white wine to help me relax and try to reassure myself the turbulence I am feeling does not mean we are going to crash, right? Closing my eyes, I lean my head against the backrest of the cramped airline seat and chronicle the events that have led to this flight, hoping a clear path forward will emerge.

Over the past ten years I have flown to California from the east coast to visit my parents for a much-needed respite from the turmoil of raising two boys. Even though there seemed to be a high level of stress between Mom and Dad as they grew older, I still looked forward to my yearly visits. They would meet me at the airport.

Mother always wore an exuberant smile, thrilled to see me. Almost before I reached the gate, I could see the child in her wanting to jump up and down with excitement. Mother never lost the wonder and love for life that eludes most people as they become mature adults. Dad was all business, rarely showing emotions, keeping a straight face. After a brief hug, "Glad you're here, Leslie. Your mother has been looking forward to your visit for weeks." Glancing at his watch, he'd continue, "Let's get your luggage, you two can talk in the car. It's costing me money to park."

Most mornings during my visit I would drive their old blue Nissan hatchback to a walking trail made possible by the removal of railroad tracks. The path stretches several miles from Lafayette to Concord. I never had the time to experience the entire trail, but I grew to relish the one hour alone along the tree-lined secluded path. On the drive back to their home, I would stop at a little coffee shop in the Village and buy a freshly brewed cup of 'Orinda blend' java. On those mornings Mother would berate me as I came through the door for spending the $2.00. "We've got coffee here," she would say. "The kettle is on the stove, and the jar of Folgers is right there in the cupboard." How I would love to hear her say those words again, just one more time.

Dad had always dreamed of creating a photography business. He took extension courses to increase his knowledge about photography, preparing for early retirement. Mom and Dad then spent a couple of years going to motorhome shows. They were seeking just the one that would suit their needs to combine travel with photography.

Dad was finally able to retire as an executive from a large department store chain at 55. He'd built a dark room for processing color film, sometimes spending 12 – 14 hours a day in that cubical creating a successful photography business in the basement of their home. He was a very young seventy-three when his cancer was discovered. "I'm sure the reason for my cancer is because of all the chemicals I've been breathing in the darkroom," Dad would tell people. "I should have known something like this would happen, I was just much too involved with the processing of my pictures." But he was optimistic about the treatment options. He didn't want surgery to remove his prostate because he didn't think he could handle the possible side-effects of impotence and incontinence. Because the cancer was in an early stage and still contained, his urologist felt radiation would be the best choice.

Weeks before the diagnosis, he had taken on the job of remodeling their master bathroom. Throughout his radiation he continued working, hammering, sawing, removing and replacing fixtures. He also enjoyed social events, and when there was something special he wanted to attend on the weekend, he skipped a couple of treatments to minimize the effects of the radiation. He wasn't going to let cancer get in his way.

After months, the final test results showed radiation had done nothing to eliminate Dad's cancer. His urologist tried all the other treatments available; female hormones (Daddy had to buy new shirts to cover his growing breasts), and experimental drugs. Two years later, while visiting us in North Carolina, I asked him, "Dad, so how are you feeling now that your treatments are finally over?"

With a couple of glasses of wine under his belt, he turned to me with a downcast, painful look on his face. "If I'd known what the last two years would be like, I would have let the cancer go without any treatment. The pain, my now defective digestive system, a lack of energy; it's just dug far too deeply into my lifestyle. Plus, I'm now impotent, something I was told *wouldn't* happen if I opted for the radiation!"

That was the first time I heard him voice feelings about the effect cancer was having on him.

"I've had to slow down and reduce my photography business," he continued. "I now have to pay someone to develop my color film. I just take the pictures."

Despite the cancer invasion, Dad worked to maintain a quality of life to show people, as well as himself, he was going to be just fine. After all, he'd explain, "That's just the way life is."

* * *

Every six months Daddy would go to the hospital to have blood drawn to check on his prostate cancer. The PSA count was always low. Only after Mother died did the score creep into the double digits. "Nothing to worry about, Clarence," said his doctor. "You are a strong, healthy man. I expect you to be around for quite some time." Every Sunday evening at seven Pacific Time, he would relay his adventures to me by phone.

Time is now drawing short for my father. Dad has spent the last twelve years running as fast as he could from the inevitable. No matter how many different treatments, hormones, experimental drugs, injections and radiation, the cancer monster continued to hover in his body . . . waiting to pounce and devour him.

* * *

The pilot's voice booms over the intercom. "Sorry folks," he announces. "There will be a thirty minute layover before we can take off again. There seems to be a light that is malfunctioning. We'll be on our way as soon as it is taken care of." Oh well, at least I'll have the opportunity to get up and walk around. Settling back into my assigned seat a few minutes later, I try to rearrange my body in the cramped space for the last leg of the trip. My knees are jammed up against the seat in front of me while a rather large woman on my right spills her over-flowing body onto my armrest. I try again to doze. The plane soon continues its journey through the dark and gloomy clouds, through the pelting rain, while I continue to sort through my recent past.

THAT'S JUST THE WAY LIFE IS...

A year ago this January, Daddy discovered blood in his urine. His urologist confirmed that his cancer had begun to spread. "It's a slow-moving cancer; no cause for alarm," he reassured Dad. "You know you'll be around for another few years, nothing to worry about!" *(Damn, why aren't doctors honest with their patients?)*

The bloody urine began leaking uncontrollably. Dad resorted to wearing large feminine pads. During this time, he discovered Elder Hostel and took a few day trips around California. He enjoyed the socializing and stimulation of learning something new.

"Daughter," he said one Sunday evening on the phone, "would you mind if I spent some of the money in my account, the account that you and your brother will be splitting when I die?"

"Of course not, Dad. What are you thinking about doing?"

"I've always wanted to travel to England, and the Elder Hostel has a three-week trip this spring. I'd like to go on that one."

"I'm so glad, Daddy. Go—and have the trip of a lifetime."

The 'leak' grew progressively worse. His urologist decided the only way Dad could make this 'trip of a lifetime' was the use of a newly devised clamp. Now mind you, I haven't a clue what this clamp looked like; my imagination can only conjure up the ugly, painful contraption. Even with this invention, Dad's one allowable suitcase was stuffed with large, bulky feminine pads. In his typical style, he'd comment in a nonchalant voice, "That's just the way life is!"

He didn't talk about the problems and discomfort he must have experienced on that trip, but I suspect it had been difficult and painful. After his return from England, Dad's doctor inserted a catheter and strapped a urine bag around his ankle. Dad continued to dance and party with a new lady friend while his urine leaked, requiring thicker pads to be worn despite the inserted catheter.

Just six months ago, as the movers were packing my china and crystal for yet another business move, Dad called me with a breathless sound in his voice. *(Cancer doesn't seem to give people time to get their lives in order.)*

"Daughter, I have been told I will have to have an ureterostomy, and the operation is scheduled for the end of this week."

"Don't worry, Dad." I sighed, "I'll be there for the surgery and stay to help you recuperate." I hung up the phone in a daze to watch the three men scattered throughout my house busily wrapping and packing my precious belongings. We were moving from New York to Massachusetts. How could I handle anything else? But I am the oldest, my brother, being seven years younger, was holding down a full-time job. Even with my lack of caregiving skills, I knew I had no choice.

Dad met me at the airport three days later. That evening I joined my brother, Bill, his wife, Kathy, Dad, and his new girlfriend, Mary, to enjoy what was called the 'last supper.' Dad ordered drinks, steak, potatoes, and a hefty dessert. "I had my pre-op today, so I am set for tomorrow. A urology nurse measured me and drew a line for the incision with a magic marker. Now I thought that was thoughtful. Want to see?"

"No, Dad, I'll just take your word for it."

"The mark is to make sure the waistband of my pants won't constrict the ureterostomy bag. Pretty nifty, don't you think?"

Even with major surgery hanging over him, Dad still maintained a sense of humor. He was laughing after returning from the men's room to empty his urine bag. "You should have seen the young boy next to me when I lifted up my pant leg at the urinal. When I saw him staring at me with huge eyes, I said, 'Be careful, young man, this could happen to you.' I am sure he relayed the incident when he returned to his family, ha, ha, ha!"

We had a lovely evening sitting outside on the restaurant's patio under an umbrella that shaded us from the afternoon sun. Dad's girlfriend was delightful with a warm, bubbly personality. She was so well maintained I thought she probably could get into her high school prom dress. Her nails were manicured, hair recently permed, and she wore a bright yellow spring dress with matching shoes. Her laugh was contagious and it rang out frequently with anything Dad had to say. They snuck quick loving glances at each other all during dinner, holding hands under the tablecloth thinking no one could see them. "Oh, we are so in love!" she remarked several times with googly eyes looking into his face. I could have sworn I was looking at two lovesick teenagers across the table from me instead of two senior citizens. *Good for my father, I thought!*

Dad explained during dinner about the surgery tomorrow. "I just can't deal with this situation any longer, and the doctor has assured me that the operation will eliminate the leaking and give me some more time to be with Mary." He was going to celebrate his 85th birthday in October and had asked Mary to honor the occasion by joining him on a cruise to the Hawaiian Islands. He was willing to grasp at anything that promised a longer life, anything to avoid the inevitable. He had always succeeded with everything he put his mind to; he was sure he was going to make it over this 'bump in the road,' as he called it.

The complicated, five-hour procedure went well, according to the doctors. Mary and I spent the time in the hospital's large, impersonal lobby. We brought along books and magazines to read, but very few pages were turned. We watched others eagerly awaiting the results of a loved one's diagnoses. Anyone who looked like he had come from the surgical area wearing greens and a mask loosely hung around his neck found us all jumping up with the same response. "Are you here for us?" "Did the surgery go well?" "Will he or she be all right?" Long after supper, after the sun had disappeared beyond the horizon, it was finally our turn to talk to the surgeon.

The doctor was quick with his response, "I don't normally attempt this surgery on an 84-year-old man, but Mr. Compton is in excellent health except for his cancer. When we opened him up, however, we discovered the urinary bladder was full of the disease, so we didn't remove it as we had hoped for fear it would escalate the cancer."

"Oh, my God," was all I could say.

"Mr. Compton's urine has been redirected to the outside of his body using a tube or catheter, which we created from a piece of his small intestine. A disposable bag surrounds the opening." Dad, he further explained, would have to learn to care for the ureterostomy and to replace the bag.

The recovery period was not a pleasant one, which we hadn't envisioned sitting around the table drinking margaritas the night before surgery. Two days after the operation an intern came to see him. "You are doing remarkably well at this point. So, you can eat anything you want on the hospital's menu." Dad took him at his word and promptly ordered waffles, syrup, and eggs for breakfast the following morning. But his poor digestive tract was not ready for such abuse. Dad's hospital stay had to be extended a few more days.

Once he was discharged, changing the urine bag became a challenging task for both of us. A home-care nurse came twice a week. She suggested we use one type of bag; the hospital nurse had insisted we use another. It didn't seem to matter which kind we tried, we just couldn't get the process down. Dad would either wake up from a nap in his recliner with urine all down the front of his pants, or he would awaken at night in a wet bed. I always knew what had happened. "DAMN!" I would hear him yell in his booming voice. No more had to be said. I was using the washing machine several times a day to keep up with the soiled clothes and linens. Eight weeks later, however, I was able to go home. Dad with his typical determination had mastered the change and care of his ureterostomy bag. It looked like he was going to make it to Hawaii with his lady after all!

Daddy had a lovely time on that cruise. He carried two cameras and took pictures of every landscape and event. I received a large envelope in the mail with photos of flowers, trees, water, the ship, and of course many lovely pictures of Mary. Even though his broad smile glowed in every photo, I could see he really wasn't looking very well. He had checked with his internist before he departed for Hawaii, because of the pain he was experiencing in his left leg. He didn't want to slow down his dancing on the ship. But the doctor told him, "Old people have poor circulation—that's all. Just take Motrin for the pain and swelling. Your leg will be fine."

* * *

As the plane nears Oakland, I am overwhelmed with conflicting emotions after last fall's experience. How will I be able to handle this new crisis? I think I'll be able to deal with the emotional aspect, but how can I care for Dad physically? I don't want to change and empty urine bags, take care of bedpans, and all the other burdens that accompany a very ill person. I found out I wasn't very good with those things last summer, never have been. Standing in the shower with my father, trying to help him replace his ureterostomy bag is not an experience I care to repeat. I resent this whole thing. I resent the intrusion on my life once again. I know I may not be able to retreat to my own home for six to twelve months! What will be left of me at that time? Who then will take care of ME? I order another glass of white wine.

My long, turbulent trip of darting in and out of storms and choppy airways, has finally ended. I am grateful my brother is meeting my plane. It will give us a chance to discuss Dad's situation. I am actually scared about seeing my father. I imagine this withered, gray, old man with oozing sores. I know he won't look that way, after all, I just saw him a few weeks ago, but I'm afraid of my reaction should my fears be realized. Walking down the runway, I am so relieved to see Bill standing heads above everyone else with his warm smile and his welcoming hug.

Unfortunately, the forty-five-minute ride from the airport is not time enough to calm my nerves. Dad greets me at his front door with a firm embrace. I can feel stress and fear in his stiffened body in that hug. His skin has an unhealthy, gray, pasty look, and he no longer emanates the vibrancy I have always associated with my father. Mentally and physically I plant my feet on the floor to prevent running out the door screaming, this can't be happening; not to my dad! My father can't die!

After dropping my suitcase in the second bedroom, the one he uses for an office, I step outside for some badly needed fresh air. I notice his backyard is now overgrown. The California poppies he had carefully nurtured last spring are crowding out the snap peas he'd planted just before winter. The neglected roses are amazingly holding one last deep red bloom. How that one flower has survived through heavy downpours is beyond me. Dad can't tend to his beloved roses, pick the peas, or even pluck lemons from the overburdened branches of his young tree. One more time I struggle not to scream. Dad has always taken great pride in the care he gives to his home; it's now deteriorating just like its owner.

I walk back through the house to his office, now a guest bedroom. I don't seem to be able to take a deep breath! This place is hot and stuffy, screaming, 'sickness, sickness' everywhere. The inside of his home also reflects Dad's declining health. In the second bathroom, I discover all the workings inside the toilet tank need to be replaced. The filter for the kitchen faucet is clogged from chemicals. Only a thin ribbon of water trickles from the spigot. Even with a housekeeper coming twice a month, grunge has collected around the countertops and inside the refrigerator. Heavy, thick, sticky dust from the gravel pit behind Dad's house has accumulated on the tops of the cabinets.

Dad tells me he can no longer do the repairs in his own home. Tuesday and Thursday evenings when I was a child, after supper, Dad would change from his suit and tie to khakis, t-shirt, and a baseball cap to go to an adult-education woodworking class. Every few weeks he'd come home with one of his latest creations. Once, two black marbleized shadow boxes appeared on the living room wall in the morning. A few weeks later there, a huge rectangular coffee table, painted a winter green, sitting on block glass legs. By the time he completed several semesters, he'd furnished the living room. The following year he designed and built furniture for my bedroom: desk, dressing table, shelves, drawers, and a radio/record player cabinet. Dad continued his projects including building an attached double garage, landscaping our beautiful yard, patio, and garden.

Now every movement seems to cause him discomfort. His left leg is swollen, unable to support his weight without the help of a wooden cane. The agony of seeing my father walking haltingly, stress and pain riddling his face, weighs me down.

I am aware that my challenge will be to distance myself from all that is going on around me in order to cope. I begin to suppress and swallow my feelings with a list of constructive chores. Work, work, keep going. Faster, faster. That's how I can deal with this. I can do the things I do best. The things Dad has taught me to do—get the essentials done. 'Don't think about it. Get on with it.' After all, as Dad would say, shrugging his shoulders, 'That's just the way life is!'

I unpack and hang up my clothes in the small closet. I blow up the air mattress laid out for me. This is where I will sleep. This will be my retreat for the next few days.

The frustration Dad feels is clearly visible on his face as he rests in his recliner. "How long is this going to go on?" he asks.

"My gut feeling is—not long, Dad."

But what really does that mean? Long enough for all of us to experience what it is we need to experience? The pendulum of the anniversary clock in his living room twists back and forth, a constant reminder of the passing of time. Breaks in the dark cumulus clouds encourage the birds to sing outside Dad's living room. A few of the residents are working in their yards; some strolling through the mobile home park to take advantage of this short reprieve in the weather. But inside everything seems dreary and stagnant. Life seems to have stopped.

Friday

Bill and I accompany Dad to his dreaded nine o'clock appointment we discussed on the phone a hundred years ago. I drive to the side entrance of the medical building to let them out at the handicap zone. Sitting silently, I watch Dad struggle with the few steps that are required, refusing the assistance Bill offers. I park the car and join them in the waiting room. The nurses at the clinic welcome Dad with warm, friendly smiles.

"Mr. Compton, how are you? So good to see you." They have seen him regularly for the past twelve years.

"Not doing very well, I'm afraid. It is probably time to call in hospice."

"Oh, you'll be okay, just think positive. You are a fighter; you'll get over this setback."

Even the doctor has smiles as he enters the exam room. Dad insists he is feeling fine except for the horrible pain in his leg. "I'm eating well, and haven't lost any weight." *How easily we try to fool ourselves. I noticed Dad's diminished appetite almost immediately.* The urologist tells us he has not looked at the bone scan, but the radiologist has told him it is cancer in Dad's left leg that is causing his swelling and pain. *I could have told him that!* He orders a series of radiation treatments. "This should make Clarence more comfortable. But unfortunately, they can't be scheduled until the middle of February," the doctor continues.

"When do we call hospice?" This time I ask the question.

"Much too soon to do that." Another broad smile appears on the doctor's face. "Hospice is only called when the expectation of survival is about six months, and I expect Clarence to be around for another year or so." He turns back to Dad. "I have made an appointment with a surgeon for you to discuss questions concerning a colostomy down the line."

Dad definitely does not want to discuss this possibility with a surgeon or anyone else. He doesn't want to go down this road!

Writing a prescription for Vicodin to ease Dad's pain, the doctor notes, "And don't forget Clarence, you can't drive while taking this medication." Daddy's cheerful smile quickly vanishes. Another slice has been taken out of his independence. His face appears to grow longer, dark shadows appearing under his eyes. Being dependent on others will be very difficult for my father. The doctor dismisses Dad with a warm smile and a hug.

"See you in three months, Clarence."

Dad decides that tonight will be his last evening as a security guard for his mobile home park. He puts the movable, magnetic security shield on his back window and the blue light on the top of his car.

"You need to be the driver tonight, Leslie. I'm experiencing too much pain in my leg. I've only taken Motrin. I don't want to fall asleep on the job.

"So, Dad, what is the routine here?"

"We need to stop at the clubhouse to get the walkie-talkie so we can communicate with home security, another volunteer, as we and another resident cruise around the park."

For the next two hours, we slowly drive up and down the rows of homes, checking in with home base to let them know everything looks secure. Dad's pain grows more intense, but he refuses to cut short his shift. My father is going downhill by the minute. I can't stop this disease from invading his body nor delay its ultimate destruction. All I can do is watch.

Sunday

Dad wants me to take him to church. A new pastor is officiating and I definitely need to make her acquaintance. I have safely locked away all my emotions the last couple of days, so I feel confident about attending the service.

The church is a very non-descript building that looks like an old barn to me, maybe it was at one time. The minister greets us on the front steps.

"So how are you doing, Clarence? Has the cancer progressed any further?"

"Yes, it has, and thanks for asking. I won't be around much longer."

As we enter the sanctuary, volunteers are placing hymnals on folding chairs arranged in a semi-circle. An upright piano is positioned at a 45-degree angle in the front. An elderly woman sits on a worn pillow she has placed on a chipped wooden bench. Kneeling pads are absent in the Unitarian Church. I miss them. I would like to be able to kneel and pray. This doesn't feel like a place of worship somehow. Maybe it is better this way. This helps me keep my emotional distance.

During the service, the minister lights a candle and says a prayer for my father. She tells the congregation about his medical condition. The floodgates I have so carefully padlocked are thrown wide open, and my raw constrained emotions come tumbling out on the floor, strong feelings I didn't know I was harboring. Tears sting my eyes as I choke back muffled sobs. All I want to do is collapse on the floor and weep. *Yes, damn it. This whole thing is shitty!* I force myself to take slow, deep breaths, staring out the window, creating pictures in the clouds fiercely collecting for another winter storm.

After the service, I watch in awe. Members of the congregation come to see my father; many had no knowledge of his condition. Never having been one to mince his words; today is no exception. With a stern, hurt face, Dad replies angrily to those who ask, "My PSA has gone up to 800. My cancer is terminal; I haven't long to live."

Standing aside, I find it fascinating to watch people's reaction to this bold statement. It's easy to see how everyone is uncomfortable with this news. They really wish they'd left the church earlier so they wouldn't have to deal with or think about this man's situation. A few parishioners giggle nervously and say, "Oh well, none of us know when our time is really up, Clarence."

Dad adamantly declares, wearing a resolved look on his face, "But I do!"

Watching him, I feel he wants to holler— "Hear me. I know life is over, death is near; my disease is terminal. There is nothing more that can be done! Why won't you listen to me? Why must you all turn away?"

But turn away they do, if not physically; mentally. They discuss the local gossip or the latest political scandal. I can feel an invisible fence being constructed around Dad so his presence won't penetrate their illusions about mortality.

Late in the afternoon, Bill and Kathy arrive at Dad's and invite me out for a quiet dinner. Mary comes over so he won't be left alone. Panicked by the sudden decline in our father's health, we begin to prioritize what needs to be done. Over dinner I explain, "You know, guys, I've got to fly home to regroup, get my life in order, re-pack so I can come back for the long haul."

"But what about my clients? They won't wait while I drive Dad around town; they'll hire someone else while you are relaxing in Massachusetts!" *I can't believe what I am hearing! What is wrong with my brother? He can always get more clients after this is all over. He needs to get his priorities in the right order!*

I clench my teeth, keeping my thoughts to myself. After all, I also have concerns. "Look, Bill, I too will be losing money. I will be spending huge amounts of money I know I don't have just to keep flying back and forth."

After dinner we apologize, aware that the word *normal* won't be a part of our vocabulary for a while and that we need to give each other more space.

My oldest son, David, has informed me he is between

assignments as an artist with Jimmy Buffett. He is flying out to help his grandfather, arriving tomorrow. Bless my son, this makes it easier for me to go back home for a couple of weeks and take the burden away from his uncle. David will sleep on the floor or the sofa in the living room, entertain his grandfather during the day, and help to keep Dad's house running.

* * *

One of my chores before I leave is to make sure my father has adequate equipment to sustain him while I am away. He needs a wheelchair and a walker. I call the urology department of Dad's HMO and ask his doctor for an equipment referral. That physician calls the medical department to have dad's regular internist authorize our requests. In turn, the internist calls the 'Durable Medical Department,' which calls in our requests to an outside company. We wait for the outside company to let us know the delivery day and time. After hours of phone calls, the outside company finally informs us it will take another two days for the items to arrive. *Where are they coming from, New York?*

In the interim, we establish routines as we wait for the medical van. To my surprise, the delivery truck arrives on time. *"This isn't so bad,"* I think, having heard horror stories about the medical system and its failures in this country.

I am prematurely pleased with their efficiency as the van heads out of the mobile home park. We scrutinize our newly delivered supplies and quickly see that a junior walker has been delivered instead of an adult one. Dad will have to walk on his knees to be able to use it! And how about that wheelchair? The wheelchair must have been produced in China in the 1920's. It is so heavy I can't lift it. And I'm the one who will need to carry it and put it in the trunk of his car when we go anywhere. I have to have something lighter, something made within the last ten years.

THAT'S JUST THE WAY LIFE IS...

The telephone is becoming my enemy. The first call I make is to the Durable Department.

"We can provide leg extensions for the walker we delivered, but to provide a new one, we'll have to go through your father's doctor for a formal request form." I begin to lose my cool. "Dad also needs a raised toilet seat. It is getting too difficult for him to get up and down," I tell the invisible female on the other end of the line.

I listen to the same pre-programmed melody over and over as she spends several minutes looking up Dad's medical records to determine what is covered under his insurance plan.

Her booming voice comes back on the line, "Oh, I am so sorry, but the toilet seat is not covered under your father's insurance." If someone has to have a wheelchair and a walker, chances are pretty good that same person will also need an elevated toilet seat! What are they thinking over there?

I can no longer be civil. "Okay, okay, I'll just go out and buy one myself! Just forget it!" I snap back at the receiver. "But I do insist on a different walker being delivered."

She tells me once again that everything must first go through them. I slam the phone into its cradle, amazed it didn't crack. Taking a couple of deep breaths, I call the 'friendly' Durable Department one more time. By now my voice is elevated, and the forced low calm that accompanied all previous requests is gone. I don't settle for the operator who answers the phone. Instead, I follow my father's style when he wants something done. "I want to speak to the supervisor, now!" I scream in my most authoritative voice.

"Don't be upset," she replies, "Ed will fix everything for you. Just call back in about an hour when he's in the office."

An hour later I'm stunned when I reach Ed on my first try. He guarantees the correct walker will be delivered. But—the wheelchair cannot be exchanged for a nice light one without the doctor's permission, because it is more expensive.

"How about a basket or carrier for the walker?" I ask.

"Oh no!" says Ed. "You can't get one of those without an examination from a physical therapist. If the PT department feels your father needs a basket attached to his walker, then she tells his doctor, who then writes a prescription to the Durable Department."

There will be no bag or basket for the front of his walker unless I buy it or make it. If I have to wade through this much red tape every time Dad needs something, he'll be dead before the requests are granted. It is my job to purchase the elevated toilet seat and the basket this afternoon.

It doesn't take long before neighbors become aware of the commotion and frustration going on in the Compton home. Answering the back door, I find one of Dad's neighbors holding, would you believe, a wheelchair. He is actually lifting it with no problem.

"I heard about some medical issues you're having over here. You can borrow this wheelchair for as long as you need it. I have no use for it anymore."

I could feel the tension in my shoulders lighten up. "Thank you so much, and your name?"

"Bruce, I live two houses down."

"Thank you, thank you, Bruce." We have a good wheelchair!

* * *

For my next errand, I head to the hospital to pick up the film and the computer printout detailing the bone scan for Dad's first radiology appointment. In the privacy of the car, I open the envelope. "My God!" I exclaim. Not only are both of Dad's legs severely affected, but he also has spots of cancer in both his arms, shoulders and back. Returning to Dad's, I retreat to the phone area and place calls to change the start date of his radiation treatment. February tenth is too long to wait.

Years ago, when someone had advanced cancer, they were

admitted to the hospital. But today there are neither the facilities nor the personnel to handle all the people afflicted with this ugly disease. Today the dying patient goes home. Someone must be there 24 hours a day, changing diapers, soiled sheets and clothes, feeding, and administering medications. I resent this burden that I must shoulder. I love my father. I've never been so close to death. I feel his anxieties, his fears, his confusion, his regrets, and his sadness surging through my body as they plague his. I don't want to go through this! I don't believe I am capable.

I'm not sure what is right anymore. I just know I can't provide all the medical supervision Dad will require. If we can afford or even find someone to care for him physically, I think I can be there for him emotionally. *I can do everything for him, rock him, hold him, cry with him; but I can't wipe his bottom!*

Two frustrating days are spent as Bill and I interview nursing and caregiving agencies. We answer ads in all the Bay Area papers. No matter what the expense, we must have someone to help us towards the end. The agencies have no one that works on a 24-hour shift, only eight hour shifts, five days a week. Each shift costs $190.00. If we go with an agency, it will mean someone different will be caring for Dad every eight hours. We don't want that, he won't stand for it.

I'm scheduled to leave for Massachusetts tomorrow. Dad is so pleased with his new walker; it allows him to get around with less assistance. He was becoming almost immobile. He also loves having his grandson around. I have his car serviced and washed, take Dad to the barber for a haircut, buy some groceries, and get some cash for him from the ATM. I alert people in his park, as well as church members, of my travel plans and ask them to look in on him during the day. I know his sweetheart will be there, and David has agreed to stay until my return. I drive Dad to HUD to sign paperwork putting his mobile home in Bill's name. My brother will take care of changing the car registration while I'm away. We're hoping these errands will avoid a hassle in the end.

All I want right now is to have my husband hold me. I need him to cradle me in his warm, loving, supportive arms so I won't feel so alone, helpless, and totally unprepared for this next chapter in our lives.

FEBRUARY

Leaf after leaf drops off, flower after flower
Some in the chill, some in the warmer hour.
Alive they flourish, and alive they fall,
And earth, who nourished them receives them all.
Should we, her wiser sons, be less content
To sink into her lap when life is spent?

Author Unknown
*(From Mother's college collection
of her favorite poems)*

First week of February

It's so good to be back home in Massachusetts, if only for a week. I am able to keep my dentist and my yearly mammogram appointments. I didn't want to reschedule, not knowing how long I would have to be in California. I feel relieved, Dad has people looking in on him while David is acting as chauffeur, cook, 'chief bottle washer,' and constant companion.

Dad gives me updates daily by phone. On Sunday evening when he calls, I inquire about his radiology treatments. "The radiologist said I should be noticing a positive change soon. He said my pain would decrease, that I'd get back some of my mobility. So far, I haven't received those promised benefits. In fact," he complains, "the pain has become more severe!"

"So David," I ask when Dad hands him the phone. "How has it been going for you, sweetheart?"

"I've been listening to Papa's records from the 30's and 40's. I'm taping all of them to take home with me as memory keepers."

I am sure my father has received immeasurable joy from hearing those old melodies and from re-telling his life stories to a new listener.

"Whenever there is a hint of sunshine," David continues, "I take Papa for long drives in the country. We put the heater on high, open the moon-roof, and play the tapes I've made from the 'oldies' in his collection, and sing at the top of our lungs."

What a delightful picture he has given me. The two are bonding in a way that can only happen in my absence. An experience my son will hold dear for the rest of his life.

"You are a very special person, David. I love you."

Monday, February 6th

Today, Dad tells me Bill drove him to an appointment with the internist because of the continued swelling in his left leg. The doctor just recommended he resume taking Motrin.

"Bill mentioned hospice again, but the doctor was quick to voice the same objection as my urologist," Dad explains. "He said I just looked too good to be very sick. By the time I got home I was feeling much better. You know, I'm not as sick as I thought I was! The radiation is going to give me more time, perhaps a weekend in Monterey with Mary. Maybe even a trip in June to Southern California for my high school reunion. I just need to be more patient." *He never saw the bone scan!*

Tuesday, February 7th

This morning, Dad calls again to tell me he just talked to the urologist. "He casually let me know he has contacted hospice and then hangs up! And only minutes after that conversation, a hospice nurse calls me to set up an appointment for *this* afternoon!" I can hear the anger in his loud, clipped voice growing faster than his cancer. "Am I worse? Why doesn't anyone tell me the truth about my condition? Why isn't anyone explaining what is going on?" *Yes, I wonder, why aren't they?*

The phone interrupts me again, this time with a message from my GYN nurse. "The doctor would like to talk with you about the results of your mammogram. Can you come in later this afternoon?" *Oh, no, this doesn't sound good.* I have been here before, three times in fact, three surgeries to find benign cells. Hopefully, this will be some of the same. I don't want to go through that trauma again.

The next phone call comes in the early afternoon. Dad's voice is back to normal; in control again. "An experienced, quiet nurse named Sharon arrived here precisely on time, gently and soothingly putting me at ease." *Thank goodness, someone who knows just how to handle someone in Dad's condition.*

Dad continues, "She said hospice isn't affiliated with my HMO. I didn't know that. If the radiation improves my condition, I can put a hold on hospice with just one phone call. And now, all my medications and medical supplies will be free, delivered right to my home." He actually sounds excited. *I'm excited and relieved.*

No more running around locating drug stores that stay open all night, calling the Durable Medical Department, waiting for physicians to write prescriptions for outside companies, fighting with hourly waged personnel about what is and what is not covered in Dad's insurance policy, and no more standing in long lines!

"Hospice is a wonderful organization," I reassure him. "And remember it's *free*. It's also the best way to get things accomplished in a reasonable amount of time. We need to use every resource that's available to make this time easier for all of us." We say our goodbyes and I slump back into my favorite chair. I need to relax, listen to the quiet, and replenish my soul before I see my doctor. But my mind won't be still. Mom died of cancer, Dad is dying of cancer, am I next?

* * *

"I'm sorry, Leslie. But your mammogram doesn't look good. I want to schedule a biopsy for you as soon as possible. You can make the appointment on your way out at the check-out counter," my doctor calmly announces from across her desk. "We see some irregularities that don't look right. We need to investigate."

"I can't do this, Doctor. I'm not going there right now . . . I can't. I have to care for my father, who is dying of cancer. It really doesn't matter what is going on with me at this time."

"It's not a good idea to put off something like this, you know."

You have no idea how well I know, I want to say to her. Instead, "I'll call when I return and make the appointment; I can't possibly have that procedure done now."

I'll return to Hayward in a couple of days, probably for the duration. I don't like Dad's home even though I helped him locate and move into the place! I don't like staying there. I can't stand the sick smell in the house. I feel guilty because I harbor this anger, yet I don't dare express it out loud. *Oh, God, don't make me go back! Why can't Dad just drop dead from a common heart attack?* All the doctors have said he has an irregular heartbeat. In fact, a couple of years ago they tested him to see if he needed to wear a pacemaker. *Why do I have to sit back and watch my father suffer?*

The winters are so romantically beautiful here. The blazing reflection from the sun on the snow crystals fills my house with light more brilliant than summer's sunshine. The warmth from the wood stove in the corner of our family room wraps around me, making me feel cozy and secure. I want to create fabric art, listen to beautiful music, and finish the book I began writing five years ago.

Why am I the one that always has to put their life on hold? I can never hold down a job because we are either transferred to a new location, or I'm putting out fires on the west coast. When will this be over? If I try to put my life in order, will the jarring ring of the phone turn my life upside down again?

This is so unfair to my father. This man runs around taking pictures, creating slideshows, organizing organ concerts, patrolling at night in his park, serving at the Elks Club, contributing to his church, and dancing and traveling with his new love. Why does all of this have to be cut short? Right in the middle of his new quest for life, he is struck down. *Yes, I am angry as Hell!*

Slowly I begin organizing and packing for my return trip to California including a couple of puzzles, several books, my needlepoint, and all my notes for the book I am writing. This will give me something to do in that gloomy atmosphere. I'll ship most of my things out ahead of time so I won't have to carry the boxes on the plane and will use Dad's computer to stay in touch with my husband daily via email. Not only will this help me feel connected to Joe, but we'll save money on our phone bills.

Wednesday, February 8th

I had an unusual dream last night. There was chaos at Dad's house. People were milling inside his home, having a grand time involved in some sort of a party. I was in his bedroom, taking care of him because he could no longer get out of bed. He suddenly had to throw up, but I couldn't get a basin to him in time. He didn't want to ruin his new mattress, so he rolled out of bed and onto the floor. I knelt down, supporting his head with a stack of towels I grabbed from his bathroom.

Surrounding us was 85 years of his accumulated stuff as well as the crowd of people making me feel very claustrophobic.

Smoothing Dad's brow as I cradled his head we talked about his life and what death meant to both of us. In different parts of the house, I could hear the sounds of laughter, music, and dancing. I cried, telling Dad I was losing my husband and my father at the same time. He too had tears streaming down his cheeks. He said he knew. He understood. There was nothing the two of us could do to change things. We held and rocked each other. I fed him some warm chicken broth, and we continued to talk as I cradled him in my arms.

Then someone brought in a huge blow-up mattress and placed it on top of his bed. I recognized the mattress—it was the same kind hospice had brought Mother at the very end of her illness.

In my dream, I somehow lost my bra and shirt. Aghast, I found I was totally exposed. Hugging my arms around my upper body, trying to maintain some modesty, I began frantically searching the room for some kind of top to wear. Anything would do. I finally found a tiny blue paisley t-shirt. It was so tight I could see my breasts and nipples. Despite the snug fit, I started cleaning out all of Dad's belongings, making him more comfortable while the others partied in the rest of the house.

* * *

My brother Bill calls in the evening. "Just wanted to let you know I interviewed a caregiver who might work out for Dad this morning. Unfortunately, English is not this candidate's native language. In fact, I can hardly understand her myself."

Three thousand miles away, I ask, "So how will Dad communicate with her, especially with his hearing problem? Aren't there any of his church people qualified to do this kind of work, any people in his mobile home park? He'll need consistency. That has always been the way he has run his life, up every morning at six, a quick shower and a shave, a choice of one of three breakfasts, and the paper. Then on to work with whatever is scheduled for the day, and he *always* adhered to a schedule: lunch at exactly noon, wine at five after the meal is prepared, supper at five-thirty, and always to bed by ten. Someone will turn up; I just know she will," I tell Bill. "We'll just keep looking. After all, we still have plenty of time before we need an extra hand."

Thursday, February 9th

I didn't sleep well last night, having a headache, upset stomach and a lot of pain in my right leg. When I awoke, I found myself wondering what I'd wear to Dad's funeral! Then more thoughts assaulted me...*I'd sure like Mom's spoon collection. Do you suppose I'll be able to split that with my sister-in-law? What about Dad's new car? It's now in Bill's name, but I sure would like David to have it after all he is doing for Dad—* How can I have thoughts like this? *Stop it! This isn't right!* Then as if my mind has a psyche of its own, I begin to plan the trips I would like to take in Dad's car after he's gone and before I return to Massachusetts!

I've heard all those profound sayings: with every ending, there is a beginning; with every death, there is a birth, and so on. But this is so final, the death of my last parent. He'll take a part of me when he goes.

Sometimes I feel like I'm going in for the kill, shifting nervously from one foot to the other, constantly glancing at my watch repeating, "Is he dead yet? Is he dead yet?"

It's a strange and somewhat guilty feeling being batted around in two different directions with no conscious thought. *God, please help me.*

THAT'S JUST THE WAY LIFE IS...

* * *

I leave for California today, and this time my husband is accompanying me on this all-day flight. Nearly all the clothes in my closet have been packed, and several boxes have been sent out ahead of my arrival. Yet it still feels like I'm not bringing enough layers to protect and shelter me.

Arriving late evening in Oakland, California, Joe and I elect to stay close to Dad's, at an old stuffy renovated 40's motel that looks like it should have been demolished years ago.

My husband spends most of his two-day visit reminiscing with his father-in-law about their fishing and camping trips every summer and the many renovating projects they did together. The two have been close for the past twenty-five years. Dad's spirits seem to brighten seeing and talking with his son-in-law again.

Dad hadn't known Joe before our wedding and was quite skeptical, not at all convinced the union would endure. But it didn't take long before a lasting relationship between the two of my favorite men began to flourish.

My father-in-law died a year after Joe and I were married. During the graveside funeral, Joe walked away from the crowd, unable to hide his grief. My father followed him. "Joe," Dad said as he gently put his hand on Joe's shoulder, "I know I can never replace your father, but I promise I will be the best substitute father I can be." Dad never faltered in his promise.

All too quickly my husband returns to Boston. Once again, I'm sleeping on the air mattress with a waffle weave foam mat tucked under the sheet in Dad's guest bedroom/office. The mattress is good—firm and supportive. But it is the old people smell from the worn-out carpet so close to my nose that stifles me. My son curls up in a sleeping bag on the living room floor or sometimes on the sofa. We put the anniversary clock in the hall closet so its chimes won't awaken him every 15 minutes.

In the morning, I inquire about a second phone line so I can email my husband without tying up the main line. There are too many calls from doctors and nurses now. I am told a second phone line, that will be active for only a short while, will cost $150!

Sunday, February 13th

Entering the kitchen this morning, Dad announces, "Even though I took my pain pills as directed last night, I had chest pains and sometimes it was difficult to take a breath."

"Why don't we try using more pillows so you're not so flat on your back? That might help, we'll try that tonight," I suggest, trying to soothe him.

Sunday greets us with the sound of torrential rain. The sky is gray, dismal, and angry. Two leaks in Dad's roof have developed because of the rivers of water spilling from the clouds. One is in Dad's bathroom, the other is over the dining room table, staining the false ceiling.

Using towels, David and I mop up the bathroom floor and then place a large saucepan to catch the constant seepage. I cover the dining room table with plastic garbage bags and put a bucket on top. Drip, drip, drip. What a mess.

Like Dad's cancer, the water is entirely out of control, and I don't know where it will show up next. Where will the next flow of water become visible on the ceiling? Which new body part will be infested with this unstoppable disease?

This afternoon is a pipe organ concert at the Berkeley High School auditorium this afternoon. Every two months, Organ clubs around the Bay Area sponsor artists to perform on this beautiful, old, outdated instrument that was painstakingly installed several years ago—one pipe at a time. Dad purchased three tickets for this concert: one for Mary, one for me, and one for himself. He demands to go to this performance despite the rain.

"Dad, I'd really rather not go in this weather. I'm concerned about driving that distance and not being able to see the road."

But there is no changing his mind. "I bought the tickets quite a while ago. Mary's looking forward to this afternoon; I don't want to disappoint her. Besides it's probably my last concert, I can't wait until the next one."

I dose Dad with Vicodin before loading him into the back seat of his car. Folding up his walker and placing it in the trunk, I put an extra urine bag in the backseat pocket and then drive the few blocks to pick up his lovely lady.

They sit together in the backseat, tenderly holding hands, cracking jokes, and laughing as though the world is full of sunshine and longevity. Dad's cheeks are sunken from loss of weight; and his color has a yellowish, jaundice cast. Odd, I didn't notice that earlier.

I refocus on my driving as I tackle the nightmarish Nimitz freeway towards Berkeley. I'm grateful most people are smart enough to stay off the roads today, while others wait patiently under overpasses for visibility to improve. But not us, oh, no! We're going to an organ concert!

Even though I'm not Catholic, I silently repeat the Rosary over and over. *Hail Mary, full of Grace, the Lord is with Thee. Blessed art thou among women. Holy Mary, mother of God, pray for us sinners now until the hour of our death.* It provides some peace, like a mantra.

The windshield wipers are a lost cause, unable to clear the windows fast enough to see anything except the deep rivers of water on the roadway. I hope no one else is driving anywhere near us; I couldn't see them if they were.

Every few minutes our car hydroplanes unexpectedly into another lane, frightening me to death. Luckily, Dad is on drugs and hasn't a clue what is happening, seeing only Mary's adoring eyes. She talks non-stop. "Oh, Clarence, we are going to have such a lovely trip to

Monterey. You know if need be, I can drive. Let's go in the spring, just a month or so from now when all the trees are in bloom."

"Wonderful, Darling. I'll begin planning this week."

My tingling, shaking hands tightly grip the steering wheel. *If we die on the road, maybe it will be easier for all of us; maybe, just maybe, we won't have to endure the next few ugly months. Maybe that's a better way to go.*

On I travel, doing about thirty miles an hour on this eight-lane freeway, seeing very little in front of me, hearing the constant swish, swish of wipers working at full speed.

Getting my father into the auditorium presents another stressful situation. I cannot let him out in the parking lot, to hobble with his walker even a few feet in this rain, he'd be drenched. Instead, I drive the car up on the sidewalk, enter the courtyard reserved for pedestrians, and head for the front entrance. Among the pointing fingers, stares, and angry voices of the seniors directed at me under their umbrellas, I park the car right next to the front door, leaving the engine running. *"Let them complain, the bastards!"* I yell inside my head. I help Dad up the steps with his walker as Mary hovers over him with her umbrella. Once Dad is safely inside, I hurry back to his illegally parked car while my hair drips rainwater into my eyes and down my coat collar, soaking my back.

Finally settled in the auditorium, I find the concert is surprisingly pleasant. The music is wonderful with melodic show tunes from the 40's and 50's. Yet, I find it difficult to relax and fully enjoy. Dad's urine bag has always made me nervous. I'm so afraid at the wrong time—hell, anytime is the wrong time—it will spring a leak like it did last summer. If it happens here, how am I going to get Dad out of his seat and to the men's room? I find my eyes roving over to his lap from time to time, but all I see are two pairs of hands entwined in companionship and love, the kind of love I never saw my parents share.

Dad takes a couple of pain pills during intermission. His friends, some of whom he has known since college, are all stunned to see this frail, stooped man dependent on a walker. "This can't be Clarence," they whisper to me. "Why, just two months ago, he was here for an organ concert and looked like his jovial self."

"What has happened, Clarence?" they inquire.

"The cancer finally got me," Daddy tells them softly, his mouth turned down in a grimace while looking at the floor. "I won't be around much longer, I'm afraid. This is probably the last concert I'll be able to attend."

"Oh come on, Clarence, you are such a fighter," friends reply. "You'll beat this setback. We'll see you in September at the big theater organ convention in Asilomar as always. And don't forget to bring your camera; it just wouldn't be the same without your good pictures."

Please God, someone be truthful with him. Someone acknowledge where he is and what he's going through, he needs that, don't they understand? He needs your support.

Dad looks exhausted after the concert, but he wants to go out for dinner. Is it because he wants to have a longer time with his lady, or just have a longer time?

"Where to, Dad?" I ask once everyone is safely settled in the car.

"Charley Brown's, that's where we're going. I want to introduce Mary to one of my favorite restaurants in the Bay Area."

Charley Brown's is at the foot of the Berkeley Marina, right on the bay, the restaurant he and Mother reserved for festive occasions.

Twilight is approaching, further diminishing the visibility of the roadway as we head towards our destination. The rain has let up only slightly, making this drive even more treacherous with the loss of light. But if Dad wants to go to Charley Brown's, then Charley Brown's it will be.

I navigate our way to the Berkeley Marina only to find Charley Brown's no longer exists. The restaurant is now part of a fast food chain with a large blinking neon sign. My father's earlier exuberant expression suddenly changes, revealing great sadness, disappointment, and betrayal. He looks like a child whose kitten has just been killed by a passing car. Something else from Daddy's life has been taken.

"Okay—okay," I hear Dad whisper. "We'll just go to one in Hayward. You like that Italian place, don't you, Mary?"

We head back to the freeway. Dad helps me negotiate through the still pelting rain, with directions to the favorite place of the Hayward Senior Citizens; an Italian restaurant owned and operated by Chinese-Americans. He takes another couple of pain pills as we settle in a booth. The restaurant is only minutes away from his home. Wine is what I want; forget the Chinese/Italian overly spicy cuisine; give me something to dull *my* pain.

Monday, February 14th

Happy Valentine's Day to someone . . . anyone?

I make an appointment at the Saturn dealership to get the windshield wipers fixed on Dad's car. They are not working at all after yesterday's adventure. Luckily, I'm able to go in later this morning. The lady who sold this car to Dad just a few months ago greets me with a warm smile when I arrive. "Where's Clarence?" she asks. "I so look forward to seeing him each time he comes in. He is such a delightful man."

"You probably didn't know this, but Dad has had prostate cancer for a several years now, and it's metastasized; it's all through his body." Her smile disappears. She, like most all of Dad's friends, had no idea there was a medical problem. "Do you by any chance, know of a caregiver who would be suitable for my father? I'm asking everyone I meet, trying to get some leads."

"You know," she says, "a couple of months ago I sold a new car to a delightful lady who is a professional, independent caregiver.

How about I get in touch with her to see if I can give you her number? I'll get right back to you as soon as I hear."

What hope she gives me! Good, qualified health professionals seem to be very few and far between.

On the drive back to Dad's house, I stop at the Lucky's grocery store near his home. I want to fix a special dinner for Dad and Mary on this Valentine's Day. He gave me twenty dollars to buy the ingredients for the recipe I've chosen. Of course twenty dollars won't go very far, but that doesn't bother me. I'll just make up the difference from my wallet; I want everything to be top quality. He doesn't ever have to know.

After purchasing what I need, including flowers and candles, I quickly return to my father's home, beginning to feel uncomfortable leaving him alone for so long. What if he falls while I'm away? Will David be able to cope with that situation?

Dad glances at my arms full of plastic grocery bags all imprinted with the Lucky's label as I come through his back door. He begins shouting at me.

"My God!" he hollers. "You didn't shop at Food for Less, where you could have purchased all those groceries for pennies?" *Yeah, right, Dad, and save what, a total of two dollars?* I am completely taken aback by this behavior.

Stamping one leg of his walker he continues. "Don't spend my money recklessly at Lucky's when Food for Less is much cheaper and the quality is a lot better. I thought you knew that!"

I try to settle him down, and in a quiet, calm voice I say, "I added my own thirty dollars to your original amount." He stops stomping his walker, becoming silent to chew on this new information and then shuffles to the living room.

It's always difficult to cook in someone else's kitchen and takes a while just to locate the simplest of ingredients and utensils. This recipe typically takes around forty-five minutes to prepare, but it is taking over an hour. And Dad's cookware is awful; some of it is cheap aluminum. It isn't long before the chef in Dad comes into the kitchen to scrutinize everything I'm doing. I open the refrigerator and take out the last item for my casserole, a hunk of Dad's favorite sharp cheddar cheese. I knew he loved the stuff, so I've bought what I had remembered to be his "special" brand.

With no warning, he really blows! For a frail, sick man, his voice lacks none of the volume it once carried when I was a child and in trouble. "Food for Less has the best cheese, and it is much less expensive. That's my favorite cheese! Why didn't you ask before you bought it?" This is the last straw. I have had it with his yelling and criticisms! *How about, 'Thank you so much for the effort and time you are taking to make this day special.'*

"This is my goddamn money and how I spend it and what I do with it is my concern." I take in a long, deep, shaky breath. "I have been working for an hour to fix a meal for you and Mary. If you were in my kitchen in Boston creating a meal for me, I certainly wouldn't treat you like you are treating me right now!" *I don't remember ever talking back to my Father.*

I put the cheese and the grater down on the counter and take firm hold of his shoulders. I speak in the calmest voice I can muster, "Do you understand now where I am coming from, Dad?"

"You're right! You're right!" he responds with a crestfallen yet resolved look and returns to the living room to be enveloped by his comfortable recliner. Despite this outburst, I know Daddy loves me. That's the reason I'm here. That's why I've elected to be with him during this time. I hold dear the memories of my early childhood, fondly recalling the fun and closeness we had together.

> Every weekday evening, when Daddy arrived home from work, he'd unfold the *Oakland Tribune*, loosen his tie, and sink into his favorite chair. Mother would serve him a hunk of sharp cheddar cheese and a jelly glass of red wine on a small tray. Sammy, our green parakeet, always joined Dad,

balancing himself on the edge of his newspaper, making it difficult to delve into any of the articles. With the wave of Daddy's hand, Sammy would quickly hop onto the edge of his glass and indulge in a little libation before finally resting on top of Dad's head to carefully preen his Brylcreemed, wavy hair. In time I'd plop myself on his lap, and after receiving my evening hug and the usual salutation of, 'Well, hello, Pumpkin,' I would ultimately begin to play with his nose.

Daddy's nose is the only one I have seen that when pressed with my finger would lay flat on his face, which fascinated me. Then, I'd convince him to once again tell me the story.

"When I was a little boy and not minding my mother," he said, "I decided to climb the forbidden old walnut tree on our ranch. I missed a limb and tumbled to the ground, breaking my nose. The only thing the doctor could do in those days was to remove the cartilage and the fragments of broken bone." We'd giggle together and he'd give me a big hug before I'd go on my way.

Reliving memories of childhood make me aware he isn't really yelling at me personally; he is lashing out at this whole damn situation because he's no longer in control. I am the only one around and represent his loss of independence and his loss of that control.

I calm down and continue putting the final touches on my dinner in anticipation of a delightful evening. I set the table with holiday napkins and the festive flower arrangement I purchased to cover the cracked veneer in the center and light the candles.

The dinner goes very well. I'm pleased both Mary and Dad seem to really enjoy my efforts to make this a special Valentine's Day for them, David even asks for seconds, so the cheese must be pretty good after all.

After dinner Dad wants to drive Mary the couple of blocks to her house to watch TV. They've watched the re-runs of *Seinfeld* every night since they began 'going steady.' Daddy doesn't care much for the program; it is just an excuse to be with his lady. "Go ahead, you two lovebirds. I'll clear the table and do the dishes, go have fun." David leaves for San Francisco to see an old friend.

With everyone out of the house, I'm able to have a little time to myself. I console my aching heart with cookies, a glass of wine, and a fast-paced murder mystery trying to forget my husband is 3,000 miles away on this Valentine's Day. *Yes, I know Daddy loves me; the yelling today has nothing to do with his real feelings for me; I'll be okay.*

Tuesday, February 15th

Dad was unable to get out of bed until nine o'clock this morning. He has never missed getting an early start to a new day. Maybe he had too much fun last night at Mary's?

"Every breath I take, my ribs hurt. I swear I can feel the cancer everywhere in my body," Dad says.

My mind quickly flashes to the images of the bone scan. It showed, among other places, cancer spots on his rib cage, that's probably what is going on. Today he's also nauseated, unable to eat his small breakfast. The last time the hospice nurse was here, she prescribed a medication to calm his stomach. I give him one of those pills, plus two more Vicodin. After an hour of sitting in his recliner, he is able to keep down a dry piece of toast.

I breathe easier knowing our nurse will be out again today to check on him. Someone to help me make decisions about Dad's care. After last night's row, I have promised myself I am going to be the very best daughter I can for him. Yet, I feel like I am moving through sticky, green, thick oil. Everything I attempt requires so much effort. I don't have the energy I am used to having. It feels like my motor and verbal skills are in slow motion, tangled with dust and cobwebs.

Whenever I sit down with Dad and talk about something of interest to me, he doesn't appear to be listening. Instead, he interrupts in mid-sentence with a recollection of a past memory, going in an all-together different direction. As Mom and Dad grew older, I noticed this pattern becoming more pronounced. As Mother aged, she formed her thoughts and ideas slower; expressing them very deliberately. Dad, who's always been in a hurry, became impatient and finished Mom's sentences before she had her thoughts collected. Mother quit trying to be heard and slowly retreated into herself. Eventually, she said almost nothing in Dad's presence. Maybe I'm supposed to be here so I can better understand Mom's side of their story; the pain and the suffering she must have endured. Once I understand, or at least am fully aware of the circumstances, what do I do then? I must be quiet and let the Spirit take over. *Take a deep breath, Leslie—keep going. Slowly breathe in and out . . . in and out; don't stop . . . in and out.*

* * *

Seeing his favorite hospice nurse, Dad actually perks up and puts on a big smile. I am so relieved to see her again. She has the perfect personality to work with my father. Dad has always needed to be the primary focus in almost all situations. This nurse lets him take the lead in their conversation. *Strange, it makes me feel a little jealous. I don't see my father light up anymore when I walk into the room.*

She calls the doctor because of Dad's chest pain, recommending a hospital bed down the line to elevate his upper body. The doctor gives his okay. "That's good, thank you. That should take care of the pain in my chest . . . Good idea," Dad says, smiling up at her from his recliner.

"However, Clarence, it will take a while for the bed to arrive. Just use several pillows to elevate your head until it does."

I'm amazed at how agreeable Dad is with this new situation. He must be having more discomfort than he has admitted to me. "But where will we put my double bed when the one from the hospital arrives? How are we going to deal with that problem?"

I convincingly tell him, "Moving your bed to the spare room will give me a better place to sleep. Then David can use the blow-up mattress on the living room floor instead of sleeping on the sofa or the floor with just a sleeping bag." Feeling he's doing us a service, Dad agrees with the plan.

My father is now taking ten Vicodin a day. The nurse tells us he's passed his limit for that drug.

"It's just too hard on Clarence's liver to be taking such large dosages. I've ordered morphine, and it'll arrive this afternoon with no charge to your father. He needs to begin taking one tablet before bed and continue the Vicodin during the day." I listen intently, writing everything down.

"Morphine sounds like I'm on my way out!" Dad roars. He certainly knows the drug represents a further decline. It's difficult for us to face his deterioration, and I can see by his expression he is trying to assimilate this disappointing information.

I walk the nurse to her car—a momentary chance to get acquainted and to breathe fresh air. This is a brief moment when I can ask someone to give me the needed 'shot in the arm' as well as a chance to talk openly about Dad's care in the very near future.

"I have been told there is a VA hospital on the peninsula that has a new hospice unit. Maybe if we don't find a caregiver, this would be the ticket. As I mentioned once before, being a caregiver is way out of the box for me. I'm really not comfortable doing this," I tell her.

She isn't enthusiastic about my idea. "If the time comes when you can't care for your father, I'll make sure there is a hospital bed for him at Kaiser." Then she adds, "Although, I know that you'll be able to keep him comfortable at home, Leslie." *I wish I were as confident about my abilities as she is.*

Even after my discussion with the nurse, the question still

haunts me; who is going to take care of Dad when I can no longer handle the situation? David is doing a fantastic job of helping out, but he too will soon wear down.

Dad spends the day napping in his recliner, but he saves enough energy to drive the two blocks to Mary's in the evening to watch television, play Tri-Ominos and indulge in some cuddling.

While Dad is at Mary's, the woman from the car dealership phones with the name and number of the caregiver she mentioned to me yesterday. I call the woman and make an appointment for tomorrow afternoon when Bill and I can meet and interview her. She sounds perfect on the phone; I pray we have finally located our special person. We haven't told Dad about our attempts to hire an experienced caregiver. Ordering morphine was enough of a jolt for him for one day.

Wednesday, February 16th

The tiresome rain continues to pelt the Bay Area. I'm sure my next project will be to build an ark. Bill meets me at Dad's and we head out for our scheduled interview with a caregiver known merely as Sam, leaving David to care for Dad's needs. Sam is working with a patient right now and has asked us to meet her outside the woman's house. We park and watch a short, buxom, red-haired, middle-aged woman bounce down the steps in the rain. She climbs into the back seat of Dad's car. We have a brief interview in this warm, dry cavern, fogging up the windows with our questions. What energy Sam has brought with her! She tells us she will be celebrating her 29th birthday next week for the 25th time. Her positive and upbeat attitude fills the small space along with a great sense of humor.

"I charge only $125.00 for a 24-hour day, but I need to be able to live in your father's home for the duration. I don't have a home of my own," she explains. "I also have a physically challenged toy poodle who hobbles around on three legs and eats only the soft food I feed him. He just sits by my feet or my patient's feet or snuggles into an available lap. He is no trouble at all."

Sam has an interesting resume. Besides being a caregiver, she has done everything from working on the first computers to driving semi-trucks across the country. Her son lives nearby, and when she's not working in a patient's home, she stays with his family—living from house to house, caring for the sick and disabled; doing the work she feels God has called her to do. "I'll cook, clean, and shop. I'm an excellent cook, don't I look it? The only thing, I won't do is yard work."

That's no big deal; I don't mind yard work, it gets me outside. Right now, she works at this address for 'Mrs. LaNasty,' as Sam calls her with a laugh. "I have given my resignation and will be available on March 29th. When this job ends, I'll be all yours, seven days a week."

This sounds wonderful. In the interim, Sam knows other people to help us if we need someone. *Okay, I can handle the situation until Sam becomes available.*

She provides three references, including a local doctor. We come to an agreement that beginning April 1st, she'll be ours. Even if we don't need her on that exact date, we'll pay her to just hang around and get acquainted with our father so she won't get tied up with anyone else. This way, Sam can have a paid break between clients and be well rested to care for Dad when the time comes.

During the drive back to Hayward, Bill and I agree to sit down with Dad and explain the reason for our absence.

"Remember when Mother was ill, Dad? We had reached a point where we could no longer care for her and ensure her comforts. We hadn't planned ahead," I remind him. "It was very difficult locating a decent caregiver on such short notice. We ended up using an agency and Mom had to deal with a different person for each eight-hour shift. Luckily, she only needed the agency for a very short while. We want to be prepared and not be left flat-footed like we were with Mom."

He accepts this explanation and seems to be comfortable with all we are doing for him right now— quietly relinquishing and entrusting his care to us.

He voices only one concern with our proposal, 'How early are we going to retain her services?' He still feels he'll be hanging in there for quite a while.

* * *

Tonight, Dad invited Mary and me to the Elks for dinner. "What a deal," Dad declares. "A steak dinner for only $4.50 and the drinks are cheap as well!"

Oh, boy. I hate going to the Elks Club. Funny, I don't think Mother would have cared for it either. Just not our 'cup of tea' she would have said. Dad mentioned a while back one of the reasons he enjoyed the Unitarian Church was the intellectual stimulation generated by so many different ideas and religions in one organization. The Elks, on the other hand, he said, is a great social outlet composed of mostly blue-collar people, many of the members living in his park. What a well-rounded life he has created for himself!

Sitting at the bar of Dad's 'social club,' he introduces me to some of his neighbors. They seem delighted to meet me, all greeting me with smiles. Everyone has had a couple of drinks, so smiles come easily. "Your dad sure works hard around here." "A pretty good cook on Saturday mornings too." Another man pipes in, "Not bad, Clarence, you also pour a hefty drink behind the counter." The praises continue. Dad can't drink, with the drugs he is taking. Passing up a glass of wine is difficult; for he has always loved a drink in the evening. But Mary and I indulge. I order another glass.

When dinner is ready, we parade into the large auditorium arranged with collapsible tables and folding chairs. Dad's face reveals the pain he is experiencing., But he's determined to have his inexpensive, Wednesday night Elks dinner. The food really isn't so bad; it's just not what I'd normally order in a restaurant or fix at home. I present my usual smiles and 'Hellos' and 'So happy to meet you' routines and order yet another glass of wine.

Seated at the table, Dad stares at his huge plate half covered by a juicy, thick steak, cooked just the way he likes it. He wants so much to eat his dinner but only manages to pick at his food, claiming that he isn't very hungry. "I'm feeling uncomfortably full and bloated tonight," he explains. I chalk up the complaint to the medication he has poured into his system.

Once again, I'm feeling nervous about that damn urine bag. What happens if it leaks, how do I handle it in here? My God. I continue to have more and more respect for this man. I don't believe I could do what he is doing. People appear more gracious here than at the organ concert, but having the same responses. No one wants to acknowledge what is happening. *Damn it, my father is dying.* I estimate the average age of this groups between the late sixties to late seventies. None of them want to look death in the eye. And Dad represents the kind of death we all dread.

We don't linger long after dessert. Dad wants to get home. He is tired, full, and not feeling well. At the same time he's quick to inform me, "Tomorrow night we are going to eat at home; Friday night Mary and I will go out to a quiet dinner alone, and Saturday night, I have planned for all of us to go to the Pizza Joint to listen to the organist who played at last Sunday's concert. He performs on a large Wurlitzer theater organ that is installed in the restaurant." *Dad will probably have to sleep all day, every day, if he intends to keep a schedule like this!*

As soon as he is settled for the night, I log onto the Internet to read my husband's email. He is my continuous support. "You'll want to reject what is to keep your dad as he was…to not have him really be there and in this situation. I wish I'd been more accepting of who my parents were in that time…to be with them as they prepared to leave their bodies behind," he wrote.

Sitting on a straight-back chair staring at the computer screen with stillness all around me, I realize I don't feel like I am really here for Dad. I am not in his space or anywhere near it. How can I be of any significant help for him? I guess I am like so many of those people I have criticized. I really don't want to face the reality of losing him. Besides, who wants to look this ugly death in the face? I certainly am not able to do that well. Just give me work and details to do, but don't open my heart to wounds and sorrows, I might lose control and be unable to function. Then what good would I be?

Whenever I received praises from Dad, it was because I took control, got things done, moved faster than other people, and did not engage in emotional feelings. I am so hopeful that Sam will be able to take some of this burden from me when she arrives.

Thursday, February 17th

This morning has given us a gift; a clear, sunny sky. After the last few days of stormy, wet weather, it's a welcome sight. Glancing out the living room window, I watch several small groups of residents socializing as they stroll around the park. I love to walk, have done so for years. It's an excellent way to begin a new day, to clear the cobwebs from the night before and get the day's events in order. But I haven't been indulging in my daily exercise, for it seems at every turn, I encounter walkers who bombard me with questions about Dad's health. Perhaps it's morbid kind of curiosity. They can play with the facts, wanting to be the first at their clubhouse to give out the gory details, but not get so close as to experience death itself. *Why don't they just call him, or better yet, go see him? Dad loves to have visitors.*

I'm tired of the daily questions; I am not walking anymore.

Dad lost his breakfast this morning. But the unexpected sunshine has brought a smile to his face. He wants to sit on the deck in his 'new' wheelchair to soak in the warmth and take a break from death for a while; listen to the birds, and watch the routines of his neighbors. But he's unable to stay focused for long, often slurring his words.

I want to know what is going on in his mind. I pull up a deck chair and sit down beside him. "Dad, are you okay with death being so close?" And, "What do you picture as the 'afterlife'?"

He responds in a very open and matter of fact manner. "I'm not sure what is next for me, but I feel certain I will continue. In what capacity I'm not sure."

"Will you please contact me when you reach 'the other side' to let me know you are all right?"

"I'll do my best."

Dad's tiring. I help him indoors and into his recliner. As he dozes I sit at his desk to read my husband's daily email. "I've made plane reservations for Jason to fly from Colorado to see his grandfather. The army is giving him special leave." Wow, another bright light in my day. My younger son is coming to visit. Dad will be so thrilled.

I'm exhausted and on edge all the time, fighting headaches. I don't seem to have the time to evaluate my life or even question the recommended breast surgery waiting for me in Massachusetts. Probably that is a good thing right now…I'm sure things will calm down soon, developing a routine that will make sense out of all the chaos.

I serve Dad his dinner early and give him the good news. "Dad," I say after he is settled in his favorite chair. "Jason is flying out to see you this weekend; the army has given him special leave time."

His face lights up, his eyes sparkle, and a big smile spreads across his face. He so adores his two grandsons.

The phone jars us from our conversation. "Hi Leslie, it's Sam. I have a few hours free this evening and would love to meet your father if he's available."

"That sounds wonderful, Sam, I'll let him know you're coming." *Fabulous!*

I clean up the kitchen and tidy the house. With a little time left, I sit down and talk to Dad about Sam and her little dog to refresh his memory. I share the reports I have received from Sam's references. "Dad, I couldn't be more impressed." I have high hopes Dad and Sam will hit it off tonight; otherwise we will be back to square one.

When Sam walks through the door, Dad welcomes her with an exuberant smile, connecting to her right away. He loves to talk about himself, and she's a willing and eager listener. Dad regales Sam with stories from his WWII navy career, his lifetime employment at H.C. Capwell department store and his many adventures as a photographer. These stories help her learn who my father really is, not the cancer that has invaded him, but the soul of the man. Spirit is really taking care of us. This lady is truly an angel sent to assist and support us through this difficult time. I quietly retreat to the computer, giving them time alone.

Friday, February 18th

This morning feels no different than the ones before it. I lie awake watching the first light of day flood my room, listening intently, holding my breath, waiting for the familiar sounds of a toilet flushing next door, the water running for a shower, telling me Dad has survived another night. Each morning he moves slower and more sluggishly through his routine. David, bless his heart, starts the coffee.

Today when Dad settles himself at the kitchen counter he complains about how full he feels again. He seems to ease his discomfort somewhat when he forces a series of burps. Unfortunately, when he burps right after his breakfast of toast and juice, his meal comes with it. I know this probably means the cancer has begun to invade his digestive system. My God, does that mean we are going to have to make a decision about IV feedings? I hope I don't have to deal with that one!

Dad has another urology appointment this morning. I'm

hoping I can settle his stomach before our drive to Oakland. This doctor has helped Dad for so many years, but I fear this time he will be out of magical potions.

When we arrive at the clinic, we are again greeted by the same nurse with the familiar welcoming smile.

"Hi, Mr. Compton, how are you doing today?" she asks in an upbeat voice.

"Not so good. Hospice was called in to help."

"Hospice—you?" The nurse quickly brushes his answer aside. "You'll get rid of that organization in no time. You don't belong with them."

Dad no longer tries to dispute such comments, just gives her a frown. He has learned it doesn't make any difference anyway. He sighs, pays his fee, and slowly maneuvers his walker to the straight back chairs arranged in a semi-circle in the waiting room.

Ushered into the exam cubicle, we soon learn the wonderful doctor has run out of options. "You know, Clarence, you need to make an appointment with the surgeon to talk about a colostomy. The cancer is invading your whole system."

Dad still refuses to make the appointment. "I'm not going down that road," he proclaims.

The urologist then dishes out the most disturbing news of all. "Clarence, the recent blood test shows your PSA count has gone up from 800 to over 1400 in five weeks. You needn't bother having this test again."

Is there anyone out there alive with a score like this? *My God, how is Dad still among the living?*

On the way home, we stop at the library in the mobile home park for some new reading material. He has always buried himself in books, devouring them by the armload.

Even with this disturbing news from the doctor, Dad insists on taking Mary out to dinner tonight as previously scheduled. She is, of course, the driver.

David invites me out to eat and to explore an area of San Francisco he has recently discovered. How very sweet of him. My son has put his life on hold to help me out and to be here for his grandfather. However, he feels he must leave by March 2nd and is concerned about how to say his goodbyes. "David, I am so sorry, but I just don't feel comfortable going to San Francisco and being an hour away from Hayward. What if Dad needs me in a hurry?"

He reluctantly settles for an Italian restaurant in town. I take my cell phone along just in case. The waiter directs us to a quiet table in a corner. I should feel a sense of relief; after all, I'm out of the house and dining with my wonderful son. He wants this to be a special evening for just the two of us. I know I must be boring company, I can't seem to talk about anything except my father. Even with two glasses of wine I gratefully consume, I can't relax. I'm continually glancing at my watch, wanting to arrive back at the house before Dad so we can help him prepare for bed and make sure he takes all his medications. And after his complaints about nausea earlier in the day, who knows how the rest of the night will turn out?

We quickly devour our meal, returning to the house only minutes before Mary brings Dad home. I meet them at the back door. My father looks like death. There is a dull, gray cast to his skin, no sparkle in his eyes, and his mouth is fixed in a grimace. He hands me his walker and the white Styrofoam box containing his uneaten pasta dinner. He carefully navigates the back, metal steps one stair at a time, not allowing either of us to help him. He is fighting this disease and his increasing dependency with all his might.

Saturday, February 19th

This morning begins a new routine. I give Dad an anti-nausea pill and a few crackers as soon as I hear him wake up. Then I leave his room so he can privately empty his overnight urine bag clipped to his bed sheet. I hear the water begin for his shower. My whole body tenses. I listen for any unusual sounds, the dropping of soap, loud moans, or the sound of a frail man falling. Today he is still able to manage alone. He shaves, dresses, and slowly maneuvers his walker to collapse exhausted into his favorite recliner. I give him an English muffin and a small glass of juice. We are both pleased; with my careful supervision, he is able to keep his breakfast down.

His phone rings, I answer it at his desk, not to bother Dad as he naps. "Mom—it's Jason."

"You're still coming tomorrow, aren't you?"

"No, Mom. That's why I'm calling. I've left the army. We were on maneuvers yesterday and I just walked off. I've had it."

"Damn you! How dare you—at a time like this! You'll never be able to tell your grandfather goodbye. He'll be so disappointed! Don't tell me where you are, because so help me if the army calls here, I will lead them to you!" I push the 'end button' and softly whisper, "Damn you. Damn you." Tears wash my face. Hanging up, I'm sure Jason has gone back to drugs, something we've had to deal with since he was fourteen. I don't think I can ever forgive him. We did everything possible to help him as he was growing up. I know I have to tell my father. I can't right now. This is all too much for me to handle.

Dad dozes off and on for three hours; yet he still complains of feeling full and bloated. I'm sure I can see the cancer cells dividing and multiplying, moving at the speed of light through his body, settling in his intestinal tract.

When he awakens, and my anger has subsided, I know I have to tell him the bad news; this is going to destroy him.

"Dad, Jason called . . . he won't be coming to see you after all. He has left the army and won't tell us where he is . . . I'm so sorry."

The sparkle fades from his eyes and his mouth turns down. No words are spoken. He works his face muscles to avoid shedding tears. He knows he will never see his young grandson again. He closes his eyes and dozes, or pretends to.

In a few minutes he complains of a nauseating feeling again.

As though reading my mind, he asks quietly. "Is it the cancer, do you think?"

"It probably is, Dad." We both understand. That is all that needs to be said. The hospice nurse won't be back until Tuesday. We'll see if she has any answers for us. Thank God we can call any time if there is an emergency.

Today my cousin Elaine and her husband Mike are driving from their home in Redding to see Dad—what a delightful welcome in this gloomy house. We laugh and talk as though life is just hunky dory! I need this respite and the relief of others, if only briefly. We talk about our childhood memories, the pranks we pulled, the secrets we shared. We laugh uproariously, relieving some of the ever-present tension surrounding us. Dad lies in his recliner half listening, half asleep. We pretend he is totally alert. Occasionally he interjects short unrelated comments. *Oh, please let's pretend for just a short while longer.* My cousin's visit is all that I had hoped it would be. I can see Dad is also pleased by the smile on his face.

Elaine and Mike say their goodbyes around four in the afternoon. Dad complains he isn't feeling well enough to go to the Pizza Joint as planned. In fact, he doesn't want to eat at all. He hasn't had anything to eat or drink since breakfast. He just grumbles about feeling painfully full.

"Unless you drink something I am going to take you to the hospital and have you put on an IV," I warn him.

More pain pills. David and I are able to get Dad to bed and asleep—hopefully for the night. I leave our bedroom door ajar so I can hear if Dad calls for me. The tenseness in my body begins to lessen as I listen to the rhythm of his breathing from the next room. Optimistically, I pretend nothing can happen as long as he is peacefully sleeping.

It is quiet and dark in the house. I love the night. Peace and space of my own. I let my thoughts wander. Dad's life hangs on a thread. I'm still holding on to that thin line of hope. But hope for what?

Sunday, February 20th

We awake again to the constant drumming of rain on the roof. I feel as though all the darkness and gloom from the heavens have descended on the Bay Area. The skies seem to be releasing tears for me because I can't.

Dad doesn't feel he can go to church today. He hates to miss the service and the socializing afterward, but he says it's just raining too hard, thank goodness. Instead, he dozes in his chair, complaining of being painfully full and bloated, not moving from the confines of his recliner. Dad manages to keep his English muffin down by forcing burps and belches. With every sound or movement he makes, I tiptoe over to check on him; so like my early days as a new mother.

After lunch there is a break in the weather. Dad's urine bag is emptied, so I'm confident he'll be okay for a while. "Dad, I just need some fresh air. Is it all right if I take a short walk? David will be here with you." He nods in the affirmative. I quickly walk the two blocks to Mary's house. I have to talk to someone; I'm at my wits' end with this new bloating problem. What's going on? How can I help? I bring the hospice phone number with me, deciding to test their 24-hour line. It will be easier to talk to a nurse away from Dad's house.

"Okay," the operator tells me after I fill her in with the details. "We will have someone come out to see your father as soon as possible."

Relief washes over me. Mary brews tea and lets me babble about nothing in particular.

When I return to Dad's I calmly tell him that I have called hospice. "Thank you," is all he can say. I'm surprised he's not upset; in fact, he seems relieved.

THAT'S JUST THE WAY LIFE IS...

Dad looks uncomfortable sitting so stiffly in his chair. He's also having trouble keeping pain medication down. He continues to force belches. He doesn't complain. He remains still and quiet, perhaps in too much pain to talk.

It's Sunday. Hospice, like all other medical services, is short on staff. 'Seeing my father right away' turns into hours of waiting. We sit together holding hands. I'm aware we wouldn't be this physically or emotionally close without this disease.

We share only occasional words, short sentences; nothing of consequence. The intermittent sound of his voice is a welcome reminder he is still with me. David fixes Jell-O and a cup of warm chicken broth, thinking his grandfather should have something to eat.

At five-thirty, an on-call hospice nurse finally arrives. We've never met her before, and it's evident from her strained look she's had a tough day. Dad's voice is now raspy. His abdomen is terribly distended, and he is very nauseous.

"Codeine causes constipation," she lectures, "particularly with inactive people. Your father's full feeling is the result of all the codeine he is taking. I'm going to increase the dosage of the stool softener and the laxative you give him each day. This will help your dad move his bowels, and he'll be just fine after that." But I think differently. I'm certain she hasn't diagnosed his condition correctly and has no clue as to what is going on.

The nurse continues directing her comments to my father. "The added laxatives will help you rest comfortably now, Mr. Compton." Her job finished, she hurries out the door to attend to her next patient.

My God, Dad is going downhill fast! I feel like I'm slipping along with him, down a long dark tunnel, falling faster and faster, like Alice falling down into the black oblivion of the rabbit's hole into unknown territory.

Two hours pass and Dad doesn't seem to be getting any relief. I have to prod and push him to take a sip of water. I sit and watch, feeling helpless, frozen in my chair next to him without a clue how to make him more comfortable.

The rain returns with its noisy clatter on the roof once again creating the water leak over Dad's bathtub. I arrange large saucepans on top of beach towels to catch the drips. Then I return to my vigil. I wait with Dad, welcoming the darkness. The dripping sound emitting from the bathtub is like a timekeeper, letting us know that drop-by-drop life is slipping away. We sit in silence.

By nine o'clock, Dad's stomach has settled a little. I'm hopeful the worst is over. Maybe we can have a peaceful night's sleep. But he is not happy about having to go to bed. He says he is much too uncomfortable to move. David and I gently help him up from his recliner, position him in his wheelchair, and slowly maneuver him to his bedroom anyway.

We prepare Dad for sleep, removing his clothes and setting up his nighttime urine bag. I fluff his pillows like Mother always did when one of us was sick, carefully adjusting them under his neck and head. As soon as he leans back however, he begins to vomit, soiling his sheets and the towels I have quickly grabbed. David is better at this than I am. For, true to my nature, I begin gagging while holding the basin just like I did with my kids. My son gently supports his grandfather's head with one hand and takes the bowl from me with the other. I have to leave the room. I am amazed how wonderfully mature my son has become. There is no way I'm going to let Dad go through this night in such pain. I call hospice again.

At eleven P.M., another nurse knocks at the door. She prescribes a different medication. Even though medication through hospice would be free, there isn't time to wait for a carrier to deliver it sometime tomorrow—I opt to go and get it. Thumbing through the phone book I locate the only pharmacy close to Dad's home that might still be open on a late Sunday night. I rush out the door leaving David in charge. Errands are so much easier for me than holding vomit bowls.

The drugstore is closing as I arrive. The manager is turning off the lights one by one. I pound on the door with both fists while pouring rain drenches my body. Putting the prescription on the windowed door so the manager can see "I'm not here to rob you," I scream, "God, please open the door!" Rushing to the front of the store, he retrieves a large round key ring from his pants pocket and carefully opens the door a crack.

"Please, can you fill this prescription for me? My father is dying and is in terrible pain."

"I can only fill this if you pay by credit card. I have already cashed out for the day." Within minutes, I have the treasured tiny pills in my hand, charging the seventy dollars to my credit card. There will be a special place in heaven for that young man.

Returning to Dad's, my shaking hands dole out the new pills with the hope of instant recovery and relief. I stay beside his bed. Five minutes pass. Twenty minutes. Thirty minutes. Dad is not improving. One more time I dial the hospice 24-hour number. With the weather and the backlog of patients, the operator informs me that no one is available for another home visit. She puts me on hold while she discusses with others on duty what should be done. Hospice decides to call in yet another prescription to an all-night pharmacy, located twenty miles away in Fremont.

I have terrible night vision and am desperately afraid of getting lost. Thankfully, David volunteers to drive even though unfamiliar with the area while I remain at Dad's bedside. David uses my credit card, charging another exorbitant amount to obtain the controlled drugs.

Dad gladly takes the magical liquid David has so gallantly obtained. I wonder if we are going to make it through the night. Will this be the medication that finally works? Exhausted, with morning only a few hours away, I silently pray. Dad leans his head against the pillows and closes his eyes. Soon he is asleep. Thankful,

David and I quietly leave Dad's bedroom.

As soon as I settle for the night the darkness envelops me. I wish I were nestled in my own bed in Massachusetts, curled against my husband, snuggled in my down comforter, escaping into blissful slumber. But sickness has changed all that. Tonight I'm experiencing some of the same anxieties I had as a child. Gloomy, scary shadows dance on the walls, laughing at my fears. The night creeps silently around me. It is deathly quiet. My rubber blow-up mattress becomes my cocoon, because we are still waiting for that magical hospital bed for Dad. *I am completely alone.*

The silence is deafening. Everyone is sleeping, fading, and becoming part of that dark void. I can hear and feel the irregularity of my own heartbeat ringing in my ears and the ever-constant ticking of the anniversary clock reminding me that time is running out. Listening for sounds of distress, I lie awake and watch the blackness spread all around me, waiting for the darkness to recede.

Monday, February 21st

The light of a new day spills into my room but I hear nothing from Dad's bedroom. I quietly tiptoe into his room, finding him awake but too uncomfortable to move. I give him pain medication, but he can't keep it down. I call hospice yet again. They promise to have a nurse out here around noon.

Will they bring any wonder drugs for me? I feel like I am walking in a trance. I know my body is running around, completing the chores and activities that keep this house in order and hopefully bringing some comfort for Dad. But I can't feel any experience of movement. My emotions and mind seem frozen in time. Dad can't hold on to life much longer. I thought I was prepared for this experience. Now I realize there was no way I could have prepared. Each day, each hour is unpredictable.

Thankfully, this next hospice nurse arrives on time. She tells us again Dad's bowels are totally blocked and gives him an enema.

"The morphine stops all bowel action when people are inactive. Morphine," she continues to explain, "is even given to young children who have persistent diarrhea."

The nurse and I settle Dad back in bed and manage to get him to sip some water. "I promise I will return tomorrow to see how you are getting along," she says with a smile as she heads for the door. Oh, how grateful I am for the wonderful people at hospice to be at our fingertips.

Dad's color improves and he seems to be resting easier, but also appears very weak after these last couple of days. Looks like he has more time after all. Of course every time we think we can relax a bit and catch our breath, something else goes haywire.

I wash several loads of towels and sheets from Dad's vomiting episodes and nurse one of my recurring headaches. With so little sleep last night, being a pill dispenser, meal preparer, clothes washer, and cleaning woman are all I am able to achieve today.

Brother Bill comes to keep us company. I welcome the emotional support he gives and know it pleases Dad when we are both here for him.

Because Dad now seems stabilized, a dear friend of mine has asked to see him and take me out to dinner. We don't travel far, just to a local pub for a beer and a sandwich. But it is so good to get away, to talk to a well human being about her job, her family, and her life. When I return, David slips out to the local video store to scour the aisles for a good movie. He chooses *Pleasantville* for our evening's entertainment. I am amazed and thrilled to watch Dad stay awake through most of the movie, his laughter filling the living room as he enjoys the show. It feels so good to see smiles cross his face. Listening to his occasional guffaws, I flash back to a time Dad and I were together when I was a child.

> Mother had a nasty cold and had been in a terrible mood all day. I was too young to know if anything else was amiss,

but the tension around our house was pretty thick. Daddy wanted to leave for the evening even after a long day at work. The local drive-in theater in El Cerrito was showing Walt Disney's *Snow White and the Seven Dwarfs*. Mom had read the story to me several times and I wanted to see the movie. But movies in my home were a luxury. They cost money, and money was only available for necessities. Dad and I were going anyway.

This was a rare treat, especially on a week night. I'd never heard my father laugh; not a real belly laugh. Usually if he found something amusing he'd smile broadly and emit a couple of "Ha, Ha's" but that was the extent. Mom always said Daddy was too serious and didn't have much of a sense of humor. Very frustrating for her, I am sure, because she found humor in most everything and accompanied it with her infectious laughter.

Daddy and I settled into one of the parking spaces. He removed the speaker box from the pole next to his window and hooked it inside. Knowing he wouldn't be able to completely roll up his window, he retrieved a wool blanket from the trunk. In no time at all we were warm and cozy inside our '37 two-door, Chevy coup, laughing at the animated comedy.

Halfway into the movie, I quit watching the screen through the car's windshield and concentrated on my father bundled up beside me. He was laughing so hard at the funny Seven Dwarfs' antics; tears were running down his cheeks. Again and again, I watched his head roll back as far as his seat would allow and come forward over the steering wheel. The car shook as his laughter filled it. He found amusement in scenes that as a youngster I didn't find very comical. Every time Dopey came on the screen, Dad began laughing all over again.

What fun I had watching this serious, purposeful, goal-orientated man laughing uproariously. What a magical evening it was! Funny, I don't remember much of the movie, just my Daddy and funny Dopey.

Tuesday, February, 22nd

Today I awake with the sound of the shower in Dad's bathroom and not the rain pounding on the roof. *Ah-ha. We must be back on track. Life will be normal again.* I quickly assemble Dad's medication and give it to him as soon as he steps out of the bathroom. His color is much improved, and after a light breakfast of English muffin and juice, he settles into his recliner.

I take a deep breath and relax a little. My headache is easing up. But during the afternoon, Dad's all too familiar full feeling returns again. His abdomen becomes painfully distended, leaving him breathless. I unpack a thousand-piece jigsaw puzzle from my suitcase to whittle away the time while Dad sleeps in his recliner. A picture of the Golden Gate Bridge with the setting sun in the background is painted on the lid of the box. I spill the pieces out on the dining room table to begin the laborious job of turning each one right side up, and searching for the straight edged pieces to frame the picture. Dad becomes concerned.

"You are filling my dining table, the only table available when I have guests in for dinner. I can't have that."

Taking a deep breath, I respond, "Dad, I promise I will immediately clear away my puzzle if Mary or anyone else comes in for a meal. It won't be a problem."

This soothes him and he goes back to sleep. The puzzle is a mindless activity. Time is momentarily suspended while I work to create an image of the bridge. This activity lets my mind roam freely, daydreaming of the way things were or the way things ought to be, loves I have lost, children I have nurtured.

The afternoon draws to a close. Dismal clouds and sheets of rain return. Dad's discomfort can no longer linger in the background of my thoughts. The jigsaw puzzle and my newest paperback murder mystery must be put aside. He hasn't been able to eat or drink since noon. His abdomen resembles a woman in her third trimester of pregnancy. "I know I won't be able to sleep tonight, I'm in too much pain," he whispers. And to prove his point, he begins vomiting. And bless David, he is right there with a bowl. At eight o'clock, feeling desperate, I call hospice again.

"No one will be able to come out to see your father until around midnight," the operator informs me. "This storm with its fierce wind is making the night difficult for our nurses; they are all running behind schedule."

I turn on the TV for a weather update to see the words dancing across the screen, "Storm warnings are up. Don't drive unless it is absolutely necessary!" I know I can't navigate Dad's car in this weather. I dial hospice once again. They decide the only option at this point is to call 911. They agree to pay for the service. I call Bill and Kathy, asking them to meet us in the emergency room.

With David's strong back, the two of us move Dad into his bedroom, where I hope he'll be more comfortable. We prop his head with pillows as he continues belching and forcing burps, hoping to stop the now continuous dry heaves. His face has grown very pale, his cheeks are sunken—he's wearing the mask of death. Very soon the *red and white taxi* (the nickname the residents have given to the ambulances that frequent their park), arrives with lights flashing. I'm sure all the neighbors are peeking through the corners of their drawn drapes and wondering who is being transported in the 'taxi' tonight. Quivering with excitement, I'm certain each one is hoping to be the first to spread the gossip in the morning.

As soon as the paramedics enter Dad's room, he sits up in bed, spreading a broad smile across his face. He scrutinizes all three men in their white uniforms.

Quickly a frown replaces the smile, but a twinkle remains in his eyes. "You come here in the middle of the night to tend to a sick and dying man and you don't bring a pretty woman with you? Where are the pretty ladies?" he scolds in mock humor.

I can't believe it. I am stunned into complete silence! Watching my father joke as they take his blood pressure and listen to his heart makes me think this is all a bad stage play. I want to go home. Nothing is wrong with my father; he just wants a little attention. He's going to be fine. As always, nothing gets this man down.

The lamp next to Dad's bed flickers as a lightning bolt flashes. The instantaneous thunder indicates a lightning strike close by, perhaps in the back yard. Torrential rain follows. The only way the paramedics are able to keep Dad from getting soaked as they transport him to the ambulance is by draping his entire body in a dark rubber tarp. Now I know his neighbors will have lots to talk about during their morning coffee klatches. Dad is also aware of this and is chuckling quietly under the tarp.

"Clarence died last night!"

"Really? Oh God, how tragic. How did he die? How do you know this?"

"Why, I was there. I saw the red and white taxi through my front window. They took him away in that dreaded body bag."

"Oh, no! I wonder if Mary knows. We better call her, better call and alert the manager, he'll need to know too. Call security, Clarence is still on patrol, isn't he?"

And on, and on it will go.

"Oh well," I say to Dad as they strap him down inside the van, "at least you've given your neighbors something different to talk about besides the weather and the persistent rain."

David drives us through Hayward, dodging the large puddles of water on the road as we follow the ambulance. I'm grateful we don't have to stop for traffic lights, just plow on ahead. Leaning back against the passenger seat, I close my eyes recalling another ambulance many years ago.

> It was a cold, rainy night, in late November, 1952. Capwell's department store had begun their Christmas hours for shoppers, extending the usual five-thirty closing time. The holiday season always put a burden on Daddy. Among other duties, he was the one who opened and closed the store. That particular Thursday night he attended an executive dinner meeting after the store closed, arriving home later than usual. I was sound asleep, but quickly awakened when I heard him come through the back door. I instinctively knew something was very wrong.
>
> I rushed out to the hallway in my long flannel nightgown carrying my baby doll close to my chest. Hiding in the shadows, I could see Daddy stretched out on the sofa in the living room. Mother was placing a blanket on top of him to warm his shivering body. I heard him admonish himself about the heavy meal he'd eaten, he should have known better, eaten just a light salad, not the pasta dish. I'd never seen Daddy sick. I didn't even remember him fighting off a cold. But there he was lying on the sofa looking worried and frightened. He began to complain that the left side of his chest and arm were giving him a lot of pain. Mother waited for Daddy's instructions before proceeding.
>
> "I think I'm having a heart attack," Daddy whispered.
>
> "What do you want me to do? I'll call the hospital and talk to a nurse."

THAT'S JUST THE WAY LIFE IS...

Mother no sooner took the four or five steps into the kitchen to make the call when Dad yelled, "Call an ambulance; forget the nurse!" Of course that is what Mother did.

Mother also called Betty, one of her best friends from church, to come and stay with 'the children.' I could see my father was in a lot of pain, he still did not complain, but even as a youngster I recognized fear mirrored in his eyes. I'd never seen my father afraid. He glanced to his side and realized I was hiding in the shadows. Stretching out his arms from under the quilt, he beckoned me to come to the sofa. With a firm grasp, he pulled me close to his chest.

"No matter what happens to me, just remember I love you, Pumpkin." Tears filled my eyes.

No one had to tell me what was taking place in my own living room—my father was dying right before my eyes! Mother, being the mother she was, told me to go back to bed, Betty would be coming to stay with me. But I didn't go to bed, how could I? I stayed in the hallway watching and listening from around the doorway.

We waited forever for the ambulance. With flashing lights, the huge white van pulled into our driveway. Two men wearing all white rolled in a gurney. Carefully they lifted Daddy onto the rolling bed and wheeled him through the front door. Mother followed in her heavy winter coat, with Phil, Betty's husband, close behind. I felt so alone. One minute life was peaceful and normal. The next minute my parents were gone with no idea of when, or if they would ever return. I slipped into my bed not because I was tired, but because Betty wasn't my mother and I didn't feel comfortable with someone I didn't know very well. Would I ever see my father again?

David stops the car behind the ambulance at the emergency entrance and I am jolted out of my reverie, realizing how Mother must have felt that rainy November evening. I am grateful; Dad will be seen ahead of the others filling the waiting room because of his arrival in an ambulance. Bill and Kathy are already there sitting together in a corner, isolating themselves from people who are coughing and sneezing. David and I join them and wait. Wait for someone to tell us something, anything about Dad's condition. Two at a time, we visit Dad in his cubicle, which has been created by drawn curtains around other patients who have arrived earlier. Dad's color is better and his voice is cheerier. Maybe it is because he feels that finally, someone will help him.

Bill and I huddle together next to Dad's bed. After only half an hour, a doctor comes into Dad's area to give his synopsis of the situation.

"Well," he says, "it sounds to me like there is either a tumor, or the colon has folded in upon itself and is blocking the works. We need to take an X-ray, Mr. Compton, to see what is actually going on."

I'm sure the doctor feels as I do; it's just the cancer doing its thing, eating up Dad's insides. Dad is wheeled down the hall to radiology. Bill and I return to the waiting room, giving Kathy and David the update.

While we wait for the results, we take turns standing by Dad's bedside, holding his hand. We talk to him about the nothings of our everyday lives, helping to pass time, filling empty spaces, relieving nervous tension.

When Dad's physician for this evening, comes down the corridor, his expression tells it all. I can literally see him composing his comments, choosing the right words to tell a waiting family of their father's imminent death. Bill and I make sure we are together with Dad when the doctor comes to relay his diagnoses.

"Mr. Compton, the X-rays show what I suspected all along.

You have either a tumor or the colon has folded in upon itself and is blocking your intestines. You have a couple of options. We can do surgery and re-route the lower intestine to the outside to a bag, called a colostomy, or you can just let it go as it is."

"So, Doctor," inquires Dad. "What will happen if I let this go? I really don't want a colostomy."

"Everything including saliva and gastric juices will be blocked. Your abdomen will continue extending and eventually the intestine will explode. We can make sure you remain comfortable with morphine, but you won't live much beyond a couple of weeks. It is a very difficult way to go down, Mr. Compton."

This is just plain shitty. Another huge chunk is ripped out of Dad's life. How must he feel? His mind is still sharp and alert but he has to experience his body dying, the disease devouring him. I can almost see the crunching bugs, like termites, chewing away on his insides.

Is Dad able to step back to look at this situation, knowing he is not his body; that his body and his Spirit will be separated but his Spirit will go on? Most of the time I try to look at this situation very logically. I know he is not really his body. But without Dad's body—?

After only a few silent minutes of deliberation, Dad elects for surgery. I am grateful in a way. I don't think I'm ready to handle the alternative. With this decision made, I begin to shake uncontrollably, suddenly chilled to the bone. My nerve endings must finally be letting go. Seeing my discomfort, Bill ushers me into the corridor while Dad continues his conversation with the doctor. I must take a badly needed break and regain some composure. As we pass the nurses' station, I hear it. Oh God, what an unbearable sound. It is my father's voice reverberating down the hallway, thundering screams accompanied by hideous retches, over and over.

"**Oh God, make it stop**," I yell, sobbing at the top of my lungs. Crying out in screeches, "I can't take this any longer, I can't stand the pain my father is going through. Oh, God, make it end." Tears stream down my face. I yell obscenities to all within earshot while slinging my open handbag across the room, hoping to slug everyone in its path.

"How dare the world treat my father this way! This is so unfair!"

My brother gently cradles me in his arms and lets me weep long and loud for all the agony and suffering we have all had to endure, for the grief and sadness that has enveloped us. My grateful body goes limp. I allow him to support me and relieve the weight I have carried these last few weeks. No security people are called. No one is yelling at me. No one is upset with me. The staff is glued in their places staring with sympathetic eyes. They all understand. Once I am reasonably calm, a nurse tells us the doctor inserted a tube down Dad's throat to remove the gastric juices from his stomach, to ensure nothing reaches the lower bowel area. "Even though the tube is very uncomfortable," she continues, "this will relieve your father's excruciating pain. He will be given oxygen and more medication to calm him down."

Bill retrieves the articles from my handbag that have spilled across the floor and we return to the waiting area. It is David and Kathy's turn to visit with Dad. Kathy is a nurse. Surely she must be better equipped emotionally to deal with this situation?

The night drags by slowly. Gurneys roll through the corridor, carrying the heart attacks, gunshot wounds, and the crazy people who have nothing better to do than to drive in this treacherous weather. In the waiting room, two young children with ear infections cry in their mothers' arms. A man in tattered clothes and no shoes talks endlessly about his days as President of the United States. An obese couple in the corner, both with long, dirty, stringy hair, gripe about the length of time it takes to see a doctor in this 'dump.' The TV in the corner blares with canned laughter, showing reruns of old sitcoms. Bill, Kathy, David, and I huddle together, feeling trapped. We are unable to get comfortable in the cheap, green stackable plastic chairs. None of us is willing to pick up a magazine from the table, not knowing who may have handled it last. Once again, I begin to numb my feelings, remembering Dad's often spoken phrase, "This is life, that's just the way life is!"

A nurse steps out of the patient holding area to tell us they won't have a room ready for Dad until three AM. We stay; taking turns visiting his bedside, watching the on-call doctor go home and another shift come aboard. The new physician informs us Dad will be given several enemas tomorrow to empty his lower bowel. In the afternoon, he will have a sigmoidoscopy. Surgery will follow when it can be scheduled.

Damn. This is difficult!

Every time I walk into his area, Dad states firmly, "Don't forget to call Mary just as soon as it's daylight."

"I will, Dad, I promise," I repeatedly have to tell him. "But I'm not going to wake her up." *Someone should be able to get some sleep tonight.* I know he's concerned the busybodies in his park will want to spread the newest gossip.

"Clarence was taken away last night by the red and white taxi in a body bag!"

Sleep certainly is not on our schedule. It's pointless. We finally leave the hospital at four AM after Dad is settled in his room, knowing we'll return in just a few hours.

Wednesday, February 23rd

I call Mary at seven forty-five.

"Mary, I am calling you before anyone else does. Dad was taken by ambulance to Kaiser last night, and will have surgery when they can schedule it. He wanted you to know."

"Let me put myself together and I'll meet you at the hospital, Leslie."

My next call is to Dad's minister. She has asked to be kept abreast of any new developments. There are three terminal parishioners she is tending to at the moment.

Walking into Dad's room an hour later, I see Mary is already there. An aide arrives and begins her chore of bathing and straightening Dad's bed. This creates a good excuse for the two of us to go downstairs, have a cup of coffee, and catch her up on some of the details. When we return, Dad's sitting up in bed and joking with the staff, making light of all that is wrong with him and telling stories about his life. Always his need to be the center of attention.

I'm living in a two-dimensional world. No wonder I enjoy puzzles so much, it resembles my life right now, no depth. I don't remember being in a situation where I've not been able to take some control. Being dyslexic, I deal with life one event or item at a time to keep panic and confusion from setting in. I don't function well in chaos. I make the rules; I do things my way. I am my father's daughter. But now I am unable to make any of the rules. I don't seem to have control over when I go to the bathroom, when I go to bed, or even when I sleep, when I can shower, when I can wash clothes, when and what I can eat.

I am completely consumed within a whirlpool swirling faster and faster, making me feel constricted, confused, and panicky. The harder I fight, the tighter and faster the ripples encircle me. If I could only let these new feelings take me where they will, I know I could cope. But old habits die hard. I've responded to stress in only one way—press on, work harder, work faster, completing tasks one at a time. I am stronger than this "cancer energy." I can win, damn it!

I spend the rest of the day sitting with Dad. Mary leaves by midday, too tired to stay, but wants to be here for his surgery. Dad is currently the only patient in a double-room affording us more privacy. Every couple of hours I go downstairs for a break and another cup of coffee.

When Joe calls me on my cell phone, my heart leaps at what he tells me. "I have a surprise for you. How about coming to the San Francisco airport around 5:30 tonight?"

"Oh, Joe, you don't know how grateful I am. Thank you." Thank God! He is such a rock for me. For a few short days I'll be able to let go of some of the stress.

The twilight darkens as black clouds open up their gates, drenching the Bay Area again. I leave Dad and drive across the San Mateo Bridge to pick up my husband at the airport, remembering the frightening adventure of hydroplaning en route to the organ concert. I am slowly getting accustomed to navigating in pouring rain with little or no visibility, trusting God will guide me along the way. *One mile at a time*, I keep reminding myself.

All incoming planes are delayed, of course, due to the weather. Joe's flight is no exception. Waiting, I sit in the lounge close to his assigned gate and order a glass of wine to calm my frayed nerves. I focus on the commuter traffic. It's relaxing, watching other people for a change, wondering what they are thinking, what schedules are going over in their minds, the loved ones they'll soon greet or the people they've left behind.

When I see my husband, all the tension literally rolls off my shoulders and I relax. I'm finally able to take a deep breath and hand over the car keys.

Joe drives us directly to the hospital. Walking into Dad's room, we find him joking with the nurse, and at the same time, complaining about how difficult it is for him to talk with the 'damn tube' down his throat. I can't look directly at him. That ugly tube is full of old, brown bubbly bile and gastric juices that are slowly being sucked out and deposited into a large, clear, glass container above his bed. I find it difficult to suppress my gagging reflexes. Instead, I stare blankly out the window, unable to watch that jar fill, praying it will be emptied in time before its contents ooze onto the floor and consume us all! I ask the nurse to please bring a towel, anything, to cover that disgusting jar.

Seeing that Dad is tiring, Joe and I head back to the car. I'm exhausted. This has been a difficult couple of days; I know I won't have trouble falling asleep tonight. Sometime between the moments I fasten my seat belt and Joe eases the car out of the hospital's parking lot, my eyes voluntarily close; I can no longer keep them open.

It is such a wonderful feeling—deep, peaceful sleep. Tonight, just one night, I don't have to anticipate hearing sounds of distress from the next room. Tonight, someone more competent than I will be caring for my father.

Thursday, February 24th

For the moment, the rain has subsided. Joe and I awaken on our air mattresses to the glorious sound of birds singing outside the window. We quickly shower and head back to the hospital for an appointment with the doctor handling Dad's case.

Entering his room at seven forty-five, we find his minister at Dad's bedside. Within minutes the doctor comes through the door. Without any discussion or 'good morning,' or even a 'hello, Mr. Compton,' he asks Dad to sign the release papers for his surgery.

"Please," I ask, "are we missing anything here? Are there other alternatives we need to be exploring?"

"No," is his reply. "Surgery should be late this afternoon or early this evening. We just have to wait in line for our number to come up." Without a smile, a handshake, or a 'How-do-you-do,' the doctor abruptly exits the room. *Where did he learn his great bedside manner?*

Dad seems to be resting comfortably. He has an IV so he isn't thirsty or hungry. The distention of his abdomen has been reduced, it's almost normal size. We all join hands as Dad's minister says a prayer for peace and comfort for my father. She wants to talk privately with Dad and asks us to leave.

Joe and I return to the mobile home, driving through another storm, to await the call to tell us the time of surgery. We stare blurry-eyed at each other from across the room, listening to the clock ring out its Westminster chime every fifteen minutes, and the return of the constant dripping of the roof leak over Dad's bathtub. We are exhausted, despite the good sleep we had last night. In the middle of the afternoon the shrill ring of the telephone jerks us back to consciousness.

"They have just given me my pill," Dad reports groggily and hangs up. I pack my needlework and a couple of magazines, knowing full well I probably won't touch them. I call Mary and tell her we'll be there to pick her up in ten minutes.

"I've been waiting. I'm all ready," she reports.

The all too familiar hospital waiting area hasn't changed since we were here for Dad's urine ostomy surgery last summer. Neither have the uncomfortable sofas clustered around the room. I'm not proud. I move a hardback chair over to where I have dropped all my belongings and set up camp. The chair will serve as my ottoman for the day. I drag another chair and put it next to the sofa. This one will hold my tote bag full of magazines and purse. Now I feel set for the duration. This is the same hospital where I gave birth to both of my boys. It was a happy time then, full of anticipation and promise.

We wait. We wait some more. Two hours. Three hours. We've been told the surgery should go rather quickly. Four hours. Small talk has been used up; only silence now is shared between the three of us. We are sure if we go out for dinner, the surgeon will show up. No one is really hungry anyway. It just would be nice to get a change of scenery. Instead, we snack on junk food from the vending machines.

It helps having Joe here, he always seems to balance life for me, and take some of the burden off my shoulders. He talks about his work schedule, friends on the east coast, hunting for our new house because the owners of our rental home are returning a year earlier than expected, and anything else he can think of to take our minds off of the present situation.

Seven-thirty PM. I see Dad's surgeon coming toward us. Even at this distance it's obvious he is a very tired man. It looks like every step is an effort, dark bags nest under his eyes.

"The surgery went well," he informs us. "However, we had a problem with all the scar tissue from his radiation, so the ostomy bag had to be placed at his belt line. It means he won't be able to wear his usual slacks. Plus the fact, I have to tell you he has cancer all through his body. I can't believe your father is still alive. He could die tomorrow. But because of his attitude and his strong desire to live, he could also surprise us and be around for another six months."

I had figured as much. But hearing a doctor verbalize this knowledge makes the facts much more real. It was no longer something I surmised; he saw the cancer invading my father! I wonder if Dad will ever be strong enough to come home again.

"Mr. Compton is in recovery now and won't be back in his room for another three hours," the doctor says, then turns to leave.

To have to sit here in this waiting room for another three hours is not even an option. Surely when Dad gets back to his room, he'll be so doped up he won't even miss us. We have to get out of here, pour some wine, be together, let down, before the next load of bricks fall.

We drive Mary home and get a take-out pizza, returning to the mobile home. Joe spends time with David while I get our beds ready. Sleep is no problem for any of us. We don't have to be alert listening for sounds of panic.

In the morning I walk around in a fog, not able to put together a full sentence. After breakfast, Joe and I drive back to the hospital wondering about Dad's condition after surgery. As soon as we enter the room he begins to verbally assault us.

"Where were you last night?!" Loudly complaining, his mouth is pulled down into his angry frown. Dad is no longer joking around. The 'fun times' are over. After all, we aren't the pretty nurses, we are just family!

"What do you mean, Dad?" I respond as gently as I can. "We were here almost all day. The surgeon came out to talk to us around seven thirty and told us you would be in recovery for at least another three hours."

Almost pleading, I continue to explain, "After the past two days, we are exhausted. Besides, I figured you would be so doped up, you wouldn't know whether we were here or not." *Wrong comment.*

"Well, you guessed wrong!" he continues in the same gruff voice, his lips knot together as though suppressing a sob. "I was back to my room in less than an hour. And I wanted you here!"

* * *

He continues to admonish us all day long as we go in and out of his room. His cutting words load me with guilt and feelings of inadequacy about the care I have given him this last month. I wish he had said, "I missed you. I so wanted you to be here for me last night, because I was scared." I could deal with those words, those feelings. I could hold him and hug him and we would have both felt better. He is pushing me further away with his hurtful words.

I am growing tired of his anger being slung in my direction. Having read Elisabeth Kubler-Ross to prepare for a grief conference years ago as a Lamaze teacher, I remember the second stage of a dying patient is anger. He has already gone through denial. At this point he obviously is bargaining, hoping for more time. But when will he finally accept his fate?

Last night is over, I'm sorry we goofed. From deep inside I want to cry out, *"Put your anger where it belongs, Dad. Yell and scream at your cancer and what it is doing to your body, but don't yell and scream at me! Hey, Dad—that's just the way life is, remember?"* At the same time, I realize my father is of another generation. A generation of men who were told not to show weaknesses, desires, emotions; to act like a *man*! My yelling back at him would accomplish nothing. I remain silent.

Later, Bill, Kathy, David, Joe, and I go out to dinner. We look for exotic foods and different wines to sample. We laugh uproariously over mundane trivia to relieve the stressful burdens we are all shouldering. There is always the hope if we laugh long and loud, drink and consume enough food, the heaviness in our chests will disappear and the overwhelming feeling of despair and sadness will abate.

Bill doesn't have a cell phone. He voices concern about his availability for emergencies, since it looks like we may continue to have a few. We all agree to get a pager for my brother and decide we will use the message of '911' to signal an emergency. This relieves some of his anxiety.

Sunday, February 27th

Too soon I am driving my husband to the San Francisco Airport. The rain is ever-present. How cruel to be separated at a time like this. Watching him walk down the runway the all too familiar feelings of aloneness and exposure begin to close in around me. I am again thrown into the whirlwind to cope by myself.

Heading back to Hayward, listening to the constant rhythmic noise of the windshield wipers, I reflect on the wonderful service hospice has provided. I play back the events of the day, keeping my mind off my husband who is flying 35,000 feet in the air toward the east coast. Today, like each day since Dad has been in the hospital, a hospice nurse came into his room to make sure he was given the proper amounts of pain medications and to check on his comfort. She always takes the time to talk and listen to him in a way hospital staff nurses, with their hectic schedules and full patient load, cannot. Today the hospice nurse spoke with me outside Dad's room, out of his earshot, to try to prepare me for the next phase of this illness.

"Your father can't last much longer," she said in a concerned whisper. "We have recommended morphine patches for him to use when he goes home. They work continually to alleviate pain. That way he will never have to be bothered taking any more pain medication."

Monday, February 28th

When I arrive at the hospital this morning, I am astonished to see Sam rather than an aide giving Dad a bath. "Sam, how good to see you. But I certainly didn't expect you so soon."

"My last patient," she explains to me, "died last week. I'm now unemployed and available for you whenever you need me. I thought this would be a good way to get better acquainted with your father and to make sure he is adequately cared for."

"Sam, how did you get all this equipment to give Dad a bath?"

"That was easy." She smiles. "I just told everyone I was Mr. Compton's private nurse and not to bother about his bath. I'll handle it each morning, and where is the storeroom?"

I was amazed to learn hospitals don't give baths anymore. It takes up too much time, and the expense of washing linens is not in their budget. Instead, they use microwave, disposable toweling and call that a bath!

She gathered real washcloths, cloth towels, soap, and a basin. Speaking to Dad softly, she puts warm water in the basin. Gently washing his weakened body, she continues talking to him in a low, comforting voice. After toweling him dry, she gives him a back rub and a foot massage with a soothing lotion first warmed in her hands.

Sam tells me she will return every evening to talk or to just sit with Mr. 'C'. This is a mutual agreement they have come to, how she will address Dad, this is how the employees at Capwell's greeted him. What a Godsend, this woman. By the time Dad returns home, he will feel very comfortable with his new caregiver.

Tuesday, February 29th

It has been a full five days since Dad's surgery. He has only been able to tolerate sips of water and broth. The assistant surgeon tried to put him on a soft diet a couple of days ago, but Dad couldn't keep any of it down. Tubes down his throat were reinserted. Now the same stupid doctor is trying to tell me Dad will be ready to go home in a couple of days!

What? I want to scream. *After all, I suppose, what can this doctor do anyway? This man is going to die shortly, so why not send him home and be rid of him, find someone else to experiment on.*

This same medical person tells me he doesn't think Dad should have the morphine patches hospice is recommending! *Who is this doctor, some kind of sadist?*

I spend the next ten minutes arguing with this crazy surgeon and get nowhere. I call my support team at hospice. We are going to do battle with this so-called physician. I may not be a medical person, but by God, I know how to make the 'powers that be' move in the right direction. Dad taught me, years ago.

Returning to my father's home, I go to work to redirect authority. I call Sam to make sure she will be available to move into Dad's house immediately. David and I dismantle Dad's double bed and move it into the guest room where I have been sleeping on the floor. I rearrange things to make the room look inviting for Sam when she arrives. I straighten up Dad's bedroom to get it ready for the delivery of that special bed hospice ordered before Dad had surgery.

When I return to the hospital I can see Dad's abdomen is distended once again. The doctor tells me not to worry, "distention is normal after surgery, it's just gas." *Right!! Something is going on in Dad's abdomen and it isn't gas!*

I take Dad for a stroll in his walker. Applauding his determination, I tell him what a great job he is doing and encourage him to walk a little further each day. During our walk, he tells me he has been instructed to do deep breathing exercises several times daily.

"Well, that seems to me like normal procedure for anyone after surgery," I reply.

"But," he confides, "it's too painful to take in deep breaths, so I'm not going to bother."

Sam discovers a bedsore on Dad's heel while bathing him. She doesn't consult a nurse. Instead she retrieves the proper medicine and a bootie for the infected foot. While soaping him down, she also discovers his colon ostomy bag is leaking. *Oh boy, here we go again!* She finds disposable gloves, calls a nurse, and begins changing his bag. *It is obvious she knows a lot more about what is going on than most of the nurses on the floor.* And the best part? She takes charge. This show of strength and knowledge gives me confidence this lady is tough and can handle *anything* that comes her way.

David says a tearful and difficult goodbye to his grandfather and leaves for the Oakland airport. He can't delay his work in Florida any longer. David assures me he'll be able to return by April first and will remain here until he is no longer needed.

Mary comes every afternoon for an hour's visit. She pulls up the only chair in the room and snuggles against his bed. They hold hands and talk about all the fun they will have at Dad's high school reunion in June. He tells her stories about his school cronies, chuckling at memories and times gone by. He is looking forward to introducing everyone to this sparkling woman who has won his heart. He tells her about the tickets he has purchased for plays to be seen later in the summer; of the fine Italian restaurant Joe and I discovered this last weekend. "If you will drive, I'll take you there," he promises. "And we'll share a smooth bottle of Merlot."

Dad receives cards every day from friends, neighbors, church members, and family. Too many of the cards spew meaningless and inappropriate well wishes all over the front flap, 'Get well, quick,' 'Hurry and get back on your feet,' 'Why, you will be up in no time.' Too many of his friends and family are still in denial. Letters arrive in the mail from people who are praying for Dad's complete recovery, even paying for candles to be lit in church to 'ensure' his recovery.

Please, I want to tell them when they call to check on Dad *Pray for a quick exit from his misery, don't stretch his suffering out any longer, there is NO cure, damn it!*

March

Boy Builder

The plane he builds with glue and wood and twine
Is frail beside the model in his brain.
And when he fails, he plans and builds again
To match the master pattern's brave design.
The ship he dreams is eagle-winged and fine;
It thunders cleanly over miles of plain,
And sky-blockading mountains pile in vain
Their peaks against it in a lofty line.
With wrinkled brow and fumbling fingertips
He maps his model on a better scheme,
And failing, then with tight determined lips
He builds another. Following the gleam,
He labors on and glues and bends and snips.
Someday his deed will match the soaring dream.

*(From Mother's college collection
of her favorite poems)*

Wednesday, March 1st

Savoring a quiet moment with a cup of tea before heading to the hospital, I read from the collection of poems Mother collected while she was in college. I smile, remembering.

Daddy loved airplanes. He and two of his closest high school friends spent many hours building model airplanes in Dad's bedroom, each, I'm sure, holding a vision about the hero he would become as a pilot. Dad's home was chosen because the two-story barn on the property proved to be the perfect place to watch their creative endeavors soar over and through the acres of orange groves. Each session the balsa gliders became more intricate. By using different woods and various glues, they hoped to build the ultimate plane to break all records for speed and duration in the air. Dad proudly displayed these successful creations on his bookshelf and dangled some from the ceiling using fishing line. Eventually one of the fellows became a pilot, and the other an aircraft engineer. Daddy had other roads to travel; but he never lost his love of airplanes and the speed of flight.

* * *

On a warm summer Sunday when I was eight months pregnant with our second son, Joe, David and I decided to go to the beach for a picnic. Joe and I were carrying the ice chest, David was lugging the paper plates, utensils and a blanket. We never opened the ice chest, never unfolded the blanket. The outing ended abruptly when Joe felt stabbing pains in his chest. The car was quickly repacked and I maneuvered my body behind the wheel to drive the two hours back home. He refused to go to any other hospital but Kaiser. Once in the Emergency room the doctor checked us both, one to make sure that the contractions I endured during the drive were not true labor and to be sure the pain Joe was experiencing was not a heart problem. The ER doctor loaded Joe with codeine and sent him home with instructions to return the following morning for more tests when the facilities would be able to accommodate him.

I called my folks as soon as we arrived home detailing the unexpected news. I needed one of them to care for our four-year-old son the following day while I accompanied Joe through the various tests. Dad came to the rescue.

Monday began like so many of the summer days east of the Berkeley hills—hot! Temperatures were predicted to hover around 95 degrees and our home had only a wall air conditioning unit in the far corner of the family room.

After getting my father settled with David's routines and the workings of the appliances, Joe and I left for the hospital. Several hours of waiting and many tests later, Joe was admitted with a collapsed lung, and a diagnosis of pleurisy.

It was late afternoon when I finally arrived home. I was hot and exhausted, longing for my favorite chair and a tall cold glass of iced tea. Stepping into our foyer I was bombarded with flying objects and cheerful laughter erupting from my son and his grandfather. The floor was layered with paper airplanes of all colors, shapes, and sizes. Some were equipped with paper clips in different sections; others donned rubber bands. Some were assembled from typing paper; others were made from construction paper in various colors. On the coffee table rested two new books detailing the creation of paper airplanes. Riotous laughter filled the hot, stuffy room. It sounded like the voices of angels to my worn out body and soul. The energy from their joy erased the fatigue I was experiencing. When the 'boys' finally noticed I had come home, their play ended. Dad's shy grin showed embarrassment at the fun he was having. But for that very brief moment I was able to snatch a glimpse of my father as a real person. Not just the breadwinner, the home repairman or the photographer; but the real man. I liked what I saw! That image helps me begin each new day.

I arrive at the hospital by eight thirty. As soon as the head surgeon enters the room, I immediately question him regarding his assistant's idea of an early dismissal.

"Oh no," the doctor replies. "You have been misinformed. Your father will not be going home in a couple of days. From the looks of things, Mr. Compton will probably be here for another week."

What a relief. I just couldn't imagine how I was going to get him home in his condition. He needs almost constant care. It looks like I'll have a few more days to unwind and gain some emotional strength for the next crisis.

Sam arrives earlier than usual. She takes him for a walk, gently bathes him, and checks on the bedsore.

An ostomy nurse is scheduled to come this morning. She wants to talk to all the members of Mr. Compton's family.

"Every family member needs to know about the care of your father's ostomy bag," she informed us yesterday.

When she arrives, I politely but firmly explain to her, "You know, I am not the one who will be dealing with either of his 'bags.' We have hired a competent caregiver to care for Dad's medical needs. I am not going to be the one to change Dad's bags."

I spill out this bit of news not only for the benefit of the ET nurse, but also to emphasize to Dad what each one of us is capable of doing. He hurls a very ugly look in my direction. It's the kind of expression that says, "I am very disappointed in you, I thought you were going to be there for me!"

"After all," he might have continued if we were alone, "The pioneers going across the country in their covered wagons never asked if they could get through tough times, they just did it! That's just the way life is!"

But a small voice inside me yells, "This is not what a daughter should do for her father." On some level, Dad must know this. My husband's email from last night helps to dissuade my guilt and strengthen that knowledge.

"Stand tough! Your role is to be there with your Dad's spirit, where he is in his moment-to-moment reality, and to serve as a conductor of talented people, friends, and relatives who are playing a human symphony for him as a thank you for all he has been for them in their lives. Let them do their work…you do yours. You already have a full time job!"

The ostomy nurse pulls Dad's hospital gown up around his chest to observe the artistry of the surgeon and discovers Dad's urine bag needs emptying. She calls for an aide to do the job. That menial task is beneath her. She continues talking to us in her authoritarian medical voice; telling Dad the reasons why the ostomy had to be located at his belt line. This information adds to his foul mood. She slips a video into the VCR and leaves us alone to watch *All There is to Know About Caring for Your Ostomy Bag!* I reluctantly watch this dumb video geared for a person who expects to change his own bag, take trips to exciting far off places, and live to be a hundred. Sam and I steal disgusted looks.

The 'exciting' movie over, the topic of 'what can Dad wear' comes up. Sam suggests hospital scrubs.

Dad brightens up and says, "I remember a catalogue I received recently. It featured, among other things, flannel slacks with drawstrings instead of a regular waistband. Go find that catalogue, Leslie, and order a few for me immediately."

It's been an hour and no one has come in to empty Dad's bag. Sam takes the incentive. She puts on disposable gloves and does the dirty job herself. Now that I have been properly schooled on the subject of ostomy bags and their care, I leave the hospital to do grocery shopping, ironing, gardening, and a general pick-up of the house.

At three-thirty as promised, a special hospital bed, nightstand, and pulley bar are delivered to Dad's house. The technician programs Dad's weight and explains the workings of this computerized mattress. Three separate areas fill up with a continuous flow of air to give the bed-ridden patient total support. He tells me the bed is also filtered to minimize odors. We unplug the bed, content that everything will be ready when Dad comes home. I drive back to the hospital.

Dad isn't doing very well with his extended stay. His skin is breaking down and his breathing has become shallow. With the constant noise in the hospital corridors; deep sleep is probably impossible. *If I were to create an environment to make it difficult for someone to recover from surgery or an illness, this is exactly how I would design it.*

"I now have a temperature of 99.9. I tried to take my afternoon walk with Sam, but that damn bedsore on my heel is too painful, as well as my left leg and foot. They are now swollen."

My sister-in-law arrives for her daily visit. Kathy quickly checks Dad over and finds his IV needs changing. The vein has begun to shut down, so he's not getting his medication. We arrange pillows to elevate his foot and feed him some of the warm broth his doctor is insisting he swallow.

Dad complains of feeling exhausted, weak, with continuous pain radiating throughout his body. His color has that gray cast again. His cheeks are sunken, and his eyes hold none of the sparkling gleam I associate with my father. I borrow a large piece of paper and a red marker from the nursing station, make a sign, and tape it to his curtain, "No Visitors allowed, except Sam." She needs to be with Dad because no one else seems to change the damn colostomy bag or the urine bag! Having her here will help him realize she is the one who will always be there when he needs medical assistance.

I pull the white nylon curtain closed around his bed and turn down the lights. I need to leave now. I know I can't do any more for him. I know he is feeling very discouraged. He knows he won't get any better. He won't ever be able to take Mary to dinner, drink his favorite wine, and whisper sweet phrases of love in her ear. He knows he won't be able to show off this person, who has given him such joy and laughter the last few months, to his cronies from high school. He is finding it too difficult to fight back. He closes his eyes, possibly to block out all that is and to imagine how it could have been.

It is dusk as I leave the hospital. Storm clouds are gathering again, foretelling of yet another impending storm. Automatic lights begin their nighttime glow up and down the street. Illuminated windows in commercial buildings highlight their after-hours' employees. On the left side of the road, a Mexican restaurant has small white Christmas lights encircling cedar trees lining their driveway. Christmas lights weave memory threads through my consciousness.

I loved the way we celebrated each Christmas. We were the stars in our own creation of a magical fairyland. We took turns exploding with laughter, emitting oohhs and aahhs while ogling over the wonderful packages piled under the tree. To lengthen our enjoyment and bathe in the spirit of the day, gifts were always wrapped individually. If several phonograph records were given, each one was in its own package designed to fool the recipient. We stretched the warm glow of togetherness, laboring over each present and carefully saving the paper and ribbon to use the following year. Our theatrical finale always ended with a chorus of, "This is the best Christmas I have ever had." Laughter and hugs always followed. Christmas—what memorable images my parents left us.

Dad's car seems to know the way to his home. I am grateful. My mind is enjoying these wanderings of happier times through all the memories of Christmas, stockpiling the pictures into one wonderful event; remembering better times.

It is very dark this early evening. The sky is filled with its wintry black clouds pelting rain on the roof. I am having trouble hearing my favorite Christmas story on the radio, *Miracle on 34th Street*. I scoot closer to the center of the old wood Philco radio cabinet, putting my ear to the upholstered speaker. Daddy should be home soon; it is Christmas Eve. Capwell's is shutting its doors on time tonight. As soon as all the last minute shoppers leave, Daddy will come home, too. Mother sits close to me in the chair with her arm around my shoulders as we listen to the many mailbags being hauled into the courtroom and dumped on the floor in front of the judge to prove once again, Kris Kringle is the *real* Santa Claus. I know this story; we listen to it every year. I pretend to be so engrossed as to not hear Daddy silently sneak into the house through the back door. I know his arms will be full of beautifully wrapped Christmas boxes. Ladies in the gift-wrapping department meticulously wrap each package just for my father. Each lid is wrapped separately with expensive paper. A huge bow created from several different ribbons adorns the center. We use these carefully wrapped boxes over again every year. Daddy stores all the magical presents in his closet at work keeping them safe until he carts them home on Christmas Eve. "After all," he tells us, while the muscles of his mouth work to control the smile wanting to emerge, "Santa doesn't come until Christmas Eve."

"Santa" silently returns to his car several times before he noisily stomps over the back door threshold to announce himself. (As though no one has heard him come in earlier!) "I've brought dinner," he calls out. The dinner is the same every Christmas Eve, but I like that, I love tradition. It lets me know nothing has changed, everything is the same as last year, it will be again next year, and next year, and the year after that, forever and ever. The food he unwraps on the kitchen counter is leftovers from the Christmas Eve luncheon the store provides for its employees. I am not sure why Daddy always gets to take home all these goodies, but it's all the delectable stuff we don't usually eat. Several different kinds of breads, ham, baloney, cheeses, fried chicken, potato salad, macaroni salad, bean salad, brownies, and See's Chocolates given to him as a gift—a regular picnic in the dead of winter and we get to eat it all.

When dinner is over, I see the tension leave Daddy's face. This time of the year is very rough on him. Capwell's begins planning Christmas in July and he has to be there every step of the way. By the time the holiday finally rolls around, he says he is sick to death of the large crowds, the extra security measures, and the long hours. But tonight and tomorrow, Dad will relax. He has completed another season and it has been a good one. He has made his figures; his contract will be renewed. A nice slow smile crosses his face as he sits in his favorite chair focusing on the blinking lights illuminating our Christmas tree, sipping a cheese glass of red wine. It is indeed good.

The dishes are soon washed and, thanks to my expert drying abilities, put away in the cupboards. Mom sits down at her piano. Flipping through a stack of books and sheet music, we know what she is looking for. A Christmas melody soon fills our living room as Mother's long delicate fingers flawlessly dance on the ivory keys. Hearing the music, Daddy goes to the hall closet to retrieve his high school violin. After a long year of sitting idle he tunes and inspects his treasured instrument. Slightly off key, he begins feeling for the correct finger positions. It only takes a couple of carols before he finds his stride. As Daddy becomes comfortable with his violin, he begins singing and harmonizing in his tenor voice. Mom joins him, singing the alto part, and whenever I know the words, I sing the melody. How wonderful to have this moment forever, every Christmas, this magical time.

Blaring sirens up ahead. I am jerked from my reverie and instantly slam on the brakes. Oh, I know this ugly neighborhood. It seems commonplace this time of night to see police cars with red lights flashing. I must be closer to Dad's mobile home park than I thought. This time though, it is worse than usual. Fresh blood is spilled on the pavement; looks like there might have been a shooting. Two ambulances arrive as well as several more police cars. It will be a while before I get through this mess.

Finally arriving at my destination, I begin to relax. The rest of the evening is mine. I park under the carport and clump-up the three stairs to the back door. Entering Dad's house, I marvel at the order of things; the personality of this place holds Dad's energy. Opening the door, I am confronted with the cheap little hat rack Dad tacked on the wall. One rung holds his red wool tartan tam he bought to go with his sports car years ago. Another rung holds his old straw fedora for summer use, another, a baseball cap from the Forbidden Palace that Joe had purchased for him during a business trip to China. There are several jackets on the other rungs, each worn to match a particular hat. They hang there just as he left them, waiting for their owner to claim them. Walking further into the living area, I am surrounded by his beautiful photographs of wildflowers, roses, birds, and trips when my parents traveled in their motor home. They fill up all the small spaces not already covered by large oil paintings. Old treasured books are stacked neatly in his bookshelves, many inherited from his father. There are full sets of Sherlock Holmes, Mark Twain, and *The History of England*; the familiar titles run across my lips. A photo album Dad prepared long ago, a chronological history of our family, rests on the coffee table he purchased with his discount from Capwell's some 45 years ago. The album has always lived in just that spot. The cabinet behind the sofa houses most of Mother's piano and organ music no one wanted after she died. A few of her favorite china cups and saucers remain in the built-in, lighted dining room cabinet.

I fondle the articles I pick up. Memories flash in my mind everywhere my eyes wander. A pad of paper, lists of frequently called phone numbers, a pen, a pencil, and a fingernail file are stacked on the small table next to his recliner. The TV remote is there, as well as the TV guide from the Sunday 'fish wrap.' I smile remembering that phrase. The residents have named the local paper the *fish wrap* to signify the importance it plays in their lives. I am careful not to disturb anything. This is the way Dad left it. If I leave these things the way I have found them, I know he will once again sit in that chair, ruffle through the papers, and make calls to people on his numerous phone lists. I want to memorize the organized clutter's position in every room, imprinting it in my mind; afraid at some point in my life I might forget. And if I fail to remember, will I then also forget my father? I can't dwell on these things; there will be time enough later.

The quiet becomes too deafening. The only noise is the hum from the refrigerator, reminding me that my "bottled refuge" is chilling. I walk the few steps to the kitchen and pour a tall glass of white wine. Returning to the living room, I settle into Mother's old rocking chair. I struggle to gain back some control by pushing the buttons on the remote, watching pictures appear on the television at my command.

Thursday, March 2nd

I call the catalog company Dad suggested and order five pair of loose fitting, drawstring pants before going to the hospital. The imbecile on the other end of the line informs me it will take two weeks for the order to be delivered.

"Two weeks! How are you shipping these, by Pony Express?" I yell into the receiver. "The man could be dead by then. If these clothes arrive after my father dies, I am returning them for a full refund!"

"Yes, of course, we will be happy to refund your money. Just send us a copy of his death certificate with your returned items." What kind of an outfit is this? If they are not going to make special allowances for my situation, then to hell with them!

I slam the phone down into its wall-mounted cradle. It feels good to be able to vent my anger. I'll deal with this later.

Driving to the hospital, I grab a cup of cappuccino from the kiosk on the outside patio and reluctantly enter Dad's room. Hopefully, I'm ready for what will greet me on the other side of his door.

He doesn't seem to be any better this morning. He is still fighting a low-grade fever. The doctor making morning rounds comes to check on him. In preparation for my father's eventual release from this place, the doctor takes him off the morphine drip. "Let's try morphine by mouth and see how that goes. I think you can handle it at this point, Mr. Compton."

Because of Dad's additional breathing problem and the swelling in his left leg and ankle, the doctor orders x-rays. The technician arrives an hour later and takes Dad down to radiology. With my responsibilities out of the way for a while, I go back to his place to freshen up for a luncheon date and shopping trip I have arranged with Mary. I need some new clothes. I have gained a few pounds with the carefully scheduled 'nutritious' meals of wine and vending machine junk food. I don't have any guilty feelings about leaving Dad alone today. He will be well cared for in my absence. Bill and Kathy are spending the afternoon with him, a gift of time so I can be on my own.

I return to the hospital at the previously agreed time of five o'clock. Walking into Dad's room, I see two freshly made empty beds with the sheets turned down! There is no evidence of anyone residing in this room; it is totally void of the energy of human life. Fearing the worst, I frantically begin running up and down the corridor shouting. "Where is Mr. Compton? Where is my father? What the hell has happened here?" It feels like an immeasurable amount of time before I find someone who has some knowledge. This shift doesn't seem to have a clue who Mr. Compton is or where he might be.

"Slow down! Mr. Compton is still in radiology," a nurse finally tells me. *This place drives me crazy!*

"Radiology!" I yell back at her. "He was taken down there early this morning. Is he still there after all this time?"

"No, of course not," another nurse chimes in. "They only x-rayed his leg this morning and he came back exhausted. He wasn't scheduled for his chest x-ray until this afternoon."

Now, this makes a whole lot of sense to me. A seriously ill old man is required to go to the radiology department two floors down, twice in one day? With a health care system this size, is there a leg technician, an arm technician, and a separate x-ray technician for the chest? A hospital is such a great place to be when one is so ill. I must be in a Frankenstein movie. Experiments are taking place two floors below me. "How can this man still be alive in his condition?" the uniformly dressed technicians ask each other. "We must locate his secret to longevity. Let's see how long he can hold out if we break him down piece by piece so he will die like the other patients around here."

The hell with this mess! I hate this place. I leave the hospital, going around the corner to a video store to rent a comedy for tonight. *Make me laugh, you fools! Make me laugh*! I am not gone long. I am back in Dad's room in thirty minutes to find him finally in his bed, as white as January's snow in Massachusetts. Every limb is shaking, his teeth are chattering. He's unable to speak because of the deep chill penetrating his body.

I search the hall and locate four blankets, pulling them off shelves. I cover him up as I would a small child, tucking the soft binding under his chin and around his neck. No words are exchanged. I hold his face in my hands and delicately kiss his forehead. He continues to shake uncontrollably for another few minutes. Looking at his face, I can see more than chill and exhaustion looming behind his eyes. This man is angry. If he had the strength, I know he would roar insults that would be heard on the next two floors.

He begins to retch from his shaking and complains of severe pain. I suddenly remember his morphine dosage was lowered, and he was taken off of the drip this morning. They must be treating him like a routine surgery patient! I can't believe this. "Let's be careful now to wean this man off of the hard drugs because he might become dependent on the stuff."

Through chattering teeth, Dad revisits his nightmare in the x-ray department. Listening to his story, heavy guilt spreads through me once again. Instead of supervising his situation, I was out having fun, enjoying lunch, and doing a little shopping.

"Bill and Kathy came to visit me this afternoon," Dad explains. "They were planning to stay for the afternoon. But an orderly came to take me down for a chest x-ray shortly after they arrived." He takes a breath in between his shakes. "They came with me as I was wheeled to radiology, then the orderly put me on a gurney. Then I was placed in the corridor to wait for an empty room and an x-ray technician. The three of us waited for a goddamn hour, so I missed my scheduled pain medication."

Dad tells me Bill and Kathy went home when he was wheeled into x-ray. They felt confident he would be in good hands. Bill and Kathy were sure Dad would be safely returned to his room when the film was processed. He continues his horror story. "I was returned to the hallway with only a sheet covering my body. I saw no one come in or out of any of the x-ray cubicles; no nurse, no orderly wandered into the empty hallway, there was just no one. No one knew I was there, no one cared."

Everyone assumed Mr. Compton had been taken back upstairs. No one bothered to check his room.

As he lay there alone in the chilly hallway pain began to consume his body. He was too weak to call out for help. Twenty minutes dragged by according to his watch, and he checked it often. Thirty minutes crawled by, forty minutes, then an hour. Daddy became chilled with his low-grade fever and the cold air blowing from the air conditioning vent directly overhead. It was an hour and a half before someone finally strolled down the hall and noticed him laying on a gurney shaking uncontrollably. They didn't have a clue where he belonged, who he was, or what he was doing there.

Tears flood my eyes, and I am consumed with anger. He continues his reflexive periodic shakes. *Goddamn it! What jerks! I am beginning to understand the situation around here.* "Oh, well, don't *have to check on that patient today, he's dying anyway. Hooray; I get to go home early!"*

I have a loud voice. I make sure everyone on staff knows what has happened to Mr. Compton today by yelling down the hall. I go to the nurse's station and insist that an IV with morphine be reinserted so he can control the amount of pain relief he needs by pushing a button. The nurse agrees with me. They are well aware I am a fuse ready to blow the place apart and cause a lot of commotion in their regimented schedule. *"We must keep the noise down, mustn't disturb the other patients."* That's the golden rule. *"And for heaven's sake, don't let anyone know what is really goes on around here."*

Dad relaxes a little, knowing he will have morphine to help relieve his pain, and with all the blankets, his shaking has stopped. Once the IV is inserted, he begins pushing the button as often as the machine will allow. He is still visibly shaken from this trauma. I can see it in his face and in his eyes—fear. Yes, fear. Something I had seen only once as a child when he had his heart attack. He is now totally dependent on others; he can no longer take care of himself, a terrible realization. He works desperately to regain some composure, some control.

Sam comes to see Dad. Bless her heart, she tells me to go home. She will stay all night if necessary, or until he is settled and feels comfortable being alone. I dial the hospital operator and ask her to hold any calls for Mr. Compton. I tape my old sign to his curtain to prevent visitors from entering. Dad continues to press the morphine button every fifteen minutes. He is comfortable with my leaving because Sam is here with him. "Sam will take care of me," he says with a small smile. And I know she will.

It is dark as I leave Dad's room around nine-thirty. I lock all the doors in his car, watching for any flashing red lights from emergency vehicles as I drive to his mobile home park. Tonight I am careful not to let my mind wander. Stepping through the back door, I suddenly feel too exhausted to watch the old comedy movie

I'd rented earlier, a movie I've seen many times before. I only have the energy to finish off the bottle of wine I opened last night.

Friday, March 3rd

I awake before 6:30, ahead of my usual schedule. Brewing a cup of Earl Grey tea, I settle into Dad's recliner and allow myself to enjoy the early morning calm. Lounging in my nightgown and robe, I open a new murder mystery and delight in thumbing through the beginning pages. At ten minutes of seven, the phone jolts me away from Dean Koontz. *Damn, I hate the phone.* Only Dad would call me at this hour, or maybe the hospital? As I grab the receiver, Dad begins a lengthy dissertation.

"Here's the latest dope. The doctor just left my room. He says that the chest x-rays taken yesterday show pleurisy. That's an infection that causes the lungs to fill with fluid and eventually collapse."

"Well, no wonder you've been experiencing so much pain when you take a deep breath, Dad. And that would explain the low-grade fever you have been having as well," I reply.

He continues his monologue. "Because of these new findings, an internist will be in later today. *You must be here* when he comes," he demands in his loud, forceful voice.

My remaining half-cup of tea has turned unappetizingly cold. I call Bill to relay the latest information. I then dial hospice to have a nurse evaluate Dad's situation. Quickly I shower and dress and retrieve the same slacks I wore yesterday from the dirty clothes bag. My calm morning is over.

I step into Dad's room at eight-thirty. Sam is busily involved in the morning routine of giving him a bath and back massage. But today, Dad is not fully enjoying her efforts. He is having trouble breathing. Each breath is accompanied with a great deal of pain. A nurse comes in and increases the amount of morphine Dad is receiving, telling us the doctor has written a new order.

With her tasks completed, Sam and I pull up a chair on either side of the bed. He's still the only patient in the room. I'm grateful for our privacy, one of the very few nice things about this place. We can use the extra bed and chairs to spread out and get reasonably comfortable. Sam reminds me she doesn't have another patient at the moment and will gladly stay until late in the afternoon.

It's incredible to watch the increased morphine go to work. Little by little Dad's color improves. The deep wrinkles around his mouth and jaw become more relaxed. He begins talking about breakfast foods. That's my father, always interested in his next meal. What he really wants this morning, he tells us with a smile, is fried eggs, bacon, pancakes, and orange juice. But Jell-O and broth are the only items brought to him.

I leave Dad's room for a cup of coffee after sitting with him for a couple of hours. I feel guilty. I should be content with a good book, catering to him, and periodically engaging in small talk. But I feel tied up and restless. There seems so little I can do for him right now. I can't seem to sit still and yet I am very exhausted. I feel like I'm dangling between two different time zones, not sure where I belong, just twirling around, dizzy, lost.

Later in the afternoon, I'm able to confer with the internist.

"Thank you so much for talking with me, Doctor. So what's really going on?"

"I don't think it is pleurisy at all." But he doesn't say what he feels the real problem is. His silence, however, tells me everything—it's the damn cancer again! The internist quietly writes another order to further elevate Dad's morphine dosage.

My favorite hospice nurse arrives shortly after the doctor leaves. After examining Dad, she ushers me into the hallway to be out of Dad's earshot. "The intense pain seems to be centered over his liver, not his lungs," she confides. No one seems to know what's really going on.

I can't talk to Dad about this. How can I tell him his cancer is totally out of control? If we could keep him under a microscope, I am sure we would see a multitude of cells dividing and multiplying. Like a movie running in fast motion, we would see these cells sent on missions throughout his body with huge ugly smirks. Or faceless demented organisms, all laughing and sounding like the wicked witch from *The Wizard of Oz* . . . "We've got you now, my pretty!"

How do you tell someone, "Oh, sorry, you have cancer in your bladder, oops, can't use that organ anymore. Oh dear, you have cancer in your lower intestine. My, my, can't use that part of your system either. Oh, my goodness, why Mr. Compton, lookie here, you have cancer in your liver and lungs. I guess you won't be using those for very long now, will you? Having any headaches lately?"

I've got to get out of this place. I'll return in a couple of hours in a different frame of mind.

Entering Dad's house, I turn the thermostat from the typical 68 to seventy-five degrees. Shakes wrack my body. I just can't seem to get warm. I pour a glass of red wine, slip my rented comedy into the VCR, and bundle up in a blanket.

Dad phones me halfway through my movie. He's afraid to go to sleep without someone with him. He's scared to close his eyes; afraid he will die. Will I please come down to the hospital and stay with him for a while? I shut off the VCR, grab my jacket, and rush back to the hospital. Still freezing, I crank up the car's heater.

Entering the hospital's garage, because it has grown dark, I search for an empty, fully lit parking space. Stepping off the elevator onto the surgical floor, I'm aware of the hospital's morgue-like atmosphere. Patients have all been medicated and are quiet; sleeping. The hall lights have been dimmed and the food carts are gone. The usual hum from the steady stream of doctors, nurses, and visitors in and out of the corridors has vanished. I spot very few staff members. It is dead quiet.

Inside Dad's room, I drag a chair close to his bedside. I hold his hand and wait quietly for him to fall asleep, listening to the muffled sounds outside of his room: An occasional laugh from a nurse, feet shuffling down the hall, and the traffic noises from the street. I wait for the morphine to win over Dad's fears so he can rest as quietly as the other patients.

Monday, March 6th

I stumbled through the weekend very much the same way I have since Dad was admitted to the hospital. This morning, however, I'm greeted by nurses outside Dad's room. "We are happy to tell you there has been a marked improvement in your father; he may be able to go home tomorrow." *I certainly didn't know he was improving.* "He's eating more, his color is better, and he's able to take a lower dosage of pain medication. The IV will be removed this afternoon and his morphine will again be administered by mouth."

Before I leave the hospital, I locate that stupid ostomy nurse who left us the delightful video last week. She never returned for it! What did she think we were going to do, watch it over and over again?

A sense of panic hovers over me like a heavy black blanket. Can't he stay just a couple more days? Soon *I* will be in charge of Dad's care, not the hospital staff. Even though we have hired Sam, I'm still the one who makes the decisions. Selfishly, I want to put off this next chapter just a little while longer. It would have been nice if he'd died in the hospital. Will he now die at home? Will I be able to handle it when he does?

Sam arrives in the early afternoon and learns of Dad's possible release from the hospital. She gives me a list of items to buy along with the food Dad has ordered. "Buy knit sheets for Mr. C. I don't mean flannel, soft knit like a t-shirt knit. Buy two sets."

I head for the shopping mall. I buy the knit sheets Sam recommends for Dad's bed and the grocery items Dad thinks he can handle. And another couple of bottles of wine for me.

Purchases paid for, I return to pack all my suitcases and boxes. I am moving out. Sam is moving in. I roll up the air mattress and foam pad. I gather up all my things spread over the house. My new place of residence will be my brother's condo. He has room for me on his living room floor. Bill and Kathy only live about 30 minutes away from Dad's place so it will be easy to come and go. Before I leave, I boot up the computer to let Joe know Dad is probably coming home tomorrow.

I arrive at my brother's doorstep looking like the homeless person I feel. Even with two suitcases, most of my clothes are stuffed into grocery bags, and liquor boxes are full of cosmetics, hair dryer, soaps, and dirty laundry. Stepping into the hallway, I am astounded at the made-over living room Kathy has so lovingly created. She purchased two stand-up screens from Cost Plus to give me some privacy and a small chest of drawers from Goodwill. Whatever doesn't fit into the chest will live in my suitcases. A bowl of fresh flowers and two delicately scented, pastel candles rest on top of the dresser. Her portable CD player is in the corner with instructions to use it any time I wish. This will be my home for the duration.

In between visits to the hospital, Sam moves into Dad's home with several suitcases, boxes, and her Toy Poodle. We will all have to learn to deal with her little dog. She rescued the poor thing from death's door and sees to his every need. He walks on three legs, has most of his buckteeth missing and spreads his terrible breath everywhere. But Sam adores him. She has promised to clean up after 'Smoo' so we'll learn to tolerate him.

Tuesday, March 7th

Camping out at Bill's should bring back fond memories. As newlyweds, Joe and I vacationed in a tent trailer. But those wonderful recollections are not blocking out my present situation. The bed is comfortable enough; it is the same mattress I used at Dad's house. I just don't have my own feeling of space and privacy.

Everyone keeps a different schedule in this house. Kathy's niece also lives here, occupying their spare bedroom. She is up at five in the morning fiddling around in the kitchen, either getting ready for work or her college classes. The screens are supposed to keep me isolated from the kitchen lights and the busy sounds of fixing breakfasts, and packing lunches. They are not working. I pull the covers up over my head; trying to pretend I don't hear the commotion. Jenny tiptoes around, I am conscious of my intrusion on her life. She turns the lights off and leaves. Silence once again.

Clomp, clomp, clomp, Bill runs down the stairs. He turns the kitchen lights back on and prepares his wife a freshly squeezed glass of orange juice and takes it upstairs.

Twenty minutes later, Kathy emerges in her bathrobe. She is showered, hair blown dry and curled, she's ready to fix her breakfast and make her lunch. She lingers over the morning paper and drinks tea from her favorite flowered cup before bounding up the stairs to finish getting ready for work.

After his wife leaves, Bill runs down the stairs once again to fix his breakfast and read a chapter in a library book. I guess that must be the signal for me to get up. After all, it is six-thirty. I can no longer delay my expected entrance into Dad's world.

I open the door of the small hall closet where I have put most of my clothes. Between the earthquake survival kit and the winter coats, I search for a clean pair of slacks. I bundle my clothes and toiletries into a bag and take them into the half bath next to the closet. Turning on the light switch, I am bombarded by the loud, rattling, vibrating exhaust fan. I begin my preparations for the day ahead. Dad is coming home today.

Joining Sam at the hospital, we watch the nurses get Dad ready for the ambulance hospice has ordered for the trip. Thank God for hospice. We follow the ambulance in separate cars. The attendants carefully carry him to his own bedroom and place him in the hospital bed I have made up with the new soft bedding. All Dad wants to do is sleep the rest of the afternoon. That's fine with us. It's getting dark. I leave Sam and Dad alone and drive back to my new accommodations on my brother's living room floor.

Wednesday, March 8th

When I open Dad's back door this morning, Sam greets me with a big smile. "Mr. C slept through the night and is feeling pretty good today! He was able to sit on the edge of his bed to eat a little breakfast." Daddy is so thrilled to be home, I can see by the light in his eyes and color in his face, it has brought new energy into his diseased body.

A short while later, 'our' hospice nurse comes for a visit. She carefully goes over instructions with Sam, the medication schedule, which ones cannot exceed the recommended dosage, and when to call hospice. After examining Dad, she quietly confides to me outside his room, "I'm concerned about your father's irregular heartbeat. I am sure his heart will finally take him out, not his cancer, which means he could go very soon." *Good. Let his heart fail him.* Why should my father have to go through any more ugliness?

Sam bathes and dresses him, helps him into his wheelchair and pushes him to his favorite recliner in the living room. At lunchtime, she wheels him up to the bar area that divides the kitchen from the family room. Dad's really bonded with his caregiver and feels God has sent her to him. The feeling is mutual. "I only care for patients God has directly sent to me," Sam declares.

More cards and flowers arrived while Dad was 'vacationing' in the hospital. Many dishes of food have been thoughtfully prepared and brought over as well. It's wonderful; we won't have to cook for a week. But the so-called 'well' people in this household are the only ones able to eat the casseroles and yummy desserts. Most of the items Dad's system won't be able to tolerate.

I spend the rest of the morning writing thank you notes to Daddy's friends for all the flowers, kind thoughts, and wonderful meals.

Mary calls. "I would like to come and visit Clarence around two. Does that work for you? Will he be able to see visitors?"

I watch my father prepare for Mary's anticipated entrance. Using his electric razor, he shaves up and down, around and around, over and over, trying to make his skin feel smooth and soft . . . just in case the two of them do some heavy duty kissing. He splashes massive amounts of aftershave lotion on his face; Mary's favorite. Using a mirror Sam holds for him, he runs a comb through his thin hair several times. Sam wheels him back to the living room and his comfortable recliner. I understand. For a very brief time, he can follow a well-written script, portray the perceived image of himself and escape the reality of his present world.

Almost all the photos I have of my father have been taken during, or right after, a production or performance. There is a picture of Dad holding his violin right after his 8th grade concert, there's one of the vocal quartets he put together to entertain his employees at Capwell's, many pictures of the numerous plays he starred in during high school and there's one showing him protesting with a group against World War II. Always the photos show a very proud and extremely pleased fellow.

In college, he was the campus photographer, taking pictures for the yearbook. He was president of different clubs and sang and acted in plays and musicals. He always seems to communicate best when he is in the limelight. Off the stage, he is lost.

I remember a comment he made to me right after he closed his photography business. "I never have any trouble in crowds of people I don't know when I have a couple of cameras around my neck. People always come to me and begin talking. The cameras have been my crutches. Without them, I don't know how to meet and talk with strangers any more. I'm always very uncomfortable."

Mary arrives for her afternoon visit while Daddy acts out the part of the proper suitor. To give them some privacy, I retreat to my puzzle laid out on the dining room table. I watch from the corner of my eye as Mary scoots a chair close to his recliner and takes his hand.

Dad working on his parent's orange ranch in Southern California, 1930's where he grew up.

THAT'S JUST THE WAY LIFE IS...

(above) Dad studying in his college library, 1935

(left) Daddy on leave, 1945

(right) Dad with his tripod and camera: The picture we chose for the cover for his memorial.

(below) Cooking Saturday breakfast for Elk's Club, 1998

(above) He loved taking pictures of wildflowers and then presenting shows for seniors.

THAT'S JUST THE WAY LIFE IS...

MR. C. E. COMPTON
Operating Superintendent
STORE MANAGER... EL CERRITO

(far right) Dad in charge of the entertainment for employees, 1950's, H.C. Capwell's.

(left) Mr. Compton Store Manager, 1957, H.C. Capwell department store.

(below) Dad spent all summer at our house with Joe, building and nurturing his garden.

LESLIE COMPTON

THAT'S JUST THE WAY LIFE IS...

(left) "What a Catch!" 1955

(below) Clearing land for the new church building.

(eight) Dad reading to his grandson, David, 1977 or 1978

(top) Mom and Dad's 60th anniversary, November, 1996

(bottom) Dad spent Christmas with us in New York, 1997

(top) Dancing with Dad at his Christmas party, 1999

(bottom) Mary and Dad beginning their Hawaiian cruise, October 1999

(top) Dad loved to cook and did so for each holiday.

(bottom) Bill and Leslie: Dad and Mom's last resting place.

Contra Costa Times: "Marian makes beautiful music," says Compton, "and I take beautiful pictures." *(1982)*

Her familiar warm giggle fills the living room, allowing my mind to wander, bringing to the forefront memories of another time.

It's picnic time again! Every summer Capwell's has a picnic providing all the food, drinks, music, and entertainment for the employees and their families. Mom doesn't want to go. She is uncomfortable in large crowds. But it is such a beautiful day; Daddy has been able to talk her into going this year after all. We have to arrive early because my father is the one in charge. He has to make sure all the committee members perform their assigned duties. Fires must be lit in the barbecue pits, the bandstand needs to be set up, and the clown hired to entertain children may require some coaching. Tables and benches have to be arranged, tablecloths spread, and the beer and soft drinks chilled. Daddy loves this. He likes being in charge, being the big cheese.

"Mr. C, where should we put the microphones?"

"Five or six fires to cook on, what do you think, will that be enough?"

"Mr. Compton, do you think we have enough beer?"

"Mr. C, was a canopy ordered to use when the sun gets too hot?"

Families begin to arrive, ready for a joyous day of activities and socializing. Daddy has already downed a couple of beers; he is ahead of most of the crowd in that department. He is enjoying himself. Mom and I are left to our own devices while he walks from area to area to put out any fires that flare up. The food is wonderful; the watermelon is chilled, sweet and juicy, just the way it should be for a picnic. The band is the same group who has performed for this occasion several years in a row; they all know Dad. He has a few more beers. As things get rolling, he grins from ear to ear. The clown is surrounded by children, hoping for either clown paint or to be tossed up in the air on a large blanket. Some of the employees have organized a softball game; others are enjoying the music and are dancing on the freshly mowed grass. This picnic is indeed a success.

Dad smiles at the musicians and steps up to the portable stage. He asks the bass player if he can take over for a while during some of the numbers. "No problem, Mr. C." Dad is once again on stage, his stage, plucking away on the thick, heavy strings, working to find the correct finger positions and notes. Every once in a while, he springs a short hop in step with the rhythm of the music or twirls the bass around on its cylindrical metal stand. He wears a huge smile on his face. I watch as the music and the roar of the crowd become my father. The more the crowd yells, 'Comp, Comp, Comp,' the faster his fingers fly across the strings. The more exaggerated his movements, the louder the crowd yells. This is their boss performing, and they love him. Daddy likes this image of himself in the limelight. I watch with awe,  pride, and adoration as the experience consumes him. "That's my father up there on that stage!"

Smiling, still hearing the cheers of the crowd, I peer around the corner of the dining room. Daddy is concentrating very hard on giving the appearance of well-being; not to nod off during their conversations from the medication. This last hospital experience has taught me I can't really relax during calm lapses like these. I have to remain alert at all times for warning signs of impending disaster. But for the moment, it looks like I might be able to take a breather.

It is eight-thirty. I'm tired. Dad's first day home from the hospital has been a good one. I leave after sampling some of the goodies left by his neighbors. I'm looking forward to my cold glass of wine when I return to my brother's. *"But please God,"* I whisper as I back out of his driveway, *"one night, just have him close his eyes and not wake up."*

Thursday, March 9th

I am beginning to establish a houseguest routine at my brother's. Each morning I get up after everyone has left for work so as to not intrude on their schedules. I dress quickly so I can detour to a coffee shop Kathy has recommended, for a latte and a sweet, low-fat muffin. I need this quiet time alone before I enter Dad's world.

A horrible smell fills my lungs, burning and tearing my eyes as I enter my father's home. Dad's bowels must really be gross! What the hell is going on now? The whole house reeks. Two steps through the doorway and Sam sends me to the drugstore to purchase several brands of colostomy pills to neutralize the odors. Dad doesn't want to repulse Mary when she comes for her visit. He wants this task to be completed instantly, two hours ago actually. "Where the hell have you been this morning, anyway? You are late!"

On the way to the pharmacy, I stop to mail two large packages home to Joe. They contain sewing projects and the pages to the book I am writing. I have no time or energy for anything creative and living at Bill's, there's no space.

I just didn't understand. I really thought I would have long quiet spells with nothing to do but write or sew while Dad rested. In retrospect, probably no one, including Dad, had any idea how this disease was going to play out.

As soon as I return from the drugstore, Sam places the pills in the ostomy bag and sprays air fresheners throughout the house, replacing the putrid smells with pine scent and cinnamon. She then begins talking at me as though it has been a lifetime since she has seen another healthy human being. I am quickly learning this place is no longer the calm, restful home it once was. This is now a nursing home for the dying. There are notebooks stacked near the phone filled with charted notes on the continued deterioration of Mr. C. Different sizes and shapes of medicine bottles line the kitchen countertop with notes dictating the time of day each is to be taken. A folded walker rests against the doorway to his bedroom, a wheelchair makes its home near Dad's recliner, and of course, the ever-present pulsating hospital bed moaning and sighing with each breath it takes.

Dad prefers to spend most of his day in the recliner. "I want to look out the window and watch my neighbors, see what they're up to. And I feel like I am still a part of this household out here." The telephone, in an easy-to-reach position, has now been added to his pencils, pens, paper, and TV remote. Everything is organized on the round table next to his chair. The phone rings often.

This afternoon, a fellow member from the Elks Lodge calls. This man writes articles for their monthly newsletter bringing members up to date on those who are ill. He has no idea why Dad was in the hospital and asks when he will see him at the Lodge again. Dad explains his situation and asks his friend to—

"Write the article telling it like it is—I went into the hospital with one bag," he laughs, "and came home with two. Now I can irrigate my garden with the original one and fertilize it with the new one!"

The poor fellow is stunned into silence. I wish I could see his expression! I am sure he won't print the article the way Dad wants; he is too baffled by these remarks. "But that's the way I want the article to run," Dad firmly states.

Before the end of the day, Dad and I spend some quiet time together. Pushing my chair closer, I take his swollen hand in mine and listen as he talks softly to me. "I believe most of my illness has been ordained and planned by a Higher Being." After a couple of breaths he continues, "And that Higher Being has also sent Sam to help me cope with my final days. I know I could die at any time, but I'm also sure the exact moment has also been pre-ordained. All we can do," he tells me, "is wait together."

On the way back to Bill's I stop at the video store and rent another movie. Kathy will be home early this evening, and we've planned to watch a chick-flick, share a bottle of wine, and eat popcorn.

Friday, March 10th

It's very interesting to watch people come and visit my father. I'm surprised by both those who make an effort and those who do not. His two sisters live in Southern California. The older sister can't come to see Dad for she is nursing her ill husband. When I asked his younger sister if she would come to see her brother, she simply stated, "I don't like to fly."

* * *

I pick up orange juice and sweet goodies at Safeway. My cousin and her husband are making their four-hour drive from Redding to see Dad again. When I arrive with refreshments, Sam is busy in the kitchen preparing Starbucks coffee on her fancy espresso machine. Dad is cleaned up, his surgical dressing is changed, and he is reclining in his favorite chair.

Our relatives arrive around nine-thirty in the morning. We

babble on about old times, the aches and pains of our elders, and the happenings of the younger generation in our families.

"Remember, Elaine, when we snuck down to Tijuana, Mexico one evening without our folks knowing? They thought we had gone to a movie!"

"Oh my goodness," Elaine remarks. "Remember how my breakfast was always Coke and Oreo cookies?"

I marvel at their show of kindness and tenderness towards my father. Sam keeps the conversation going as Dad dozes and occasionally joins in with a, "Yeah, for sure," "That's right," or "Glad to hear it." He doesn't seem able to put much of a sentence together. I wonder if his visitors are taxing him too much. Or does he wish his guests would hurry on their way? We are supposed to be entertaining and visiting with Dad. I wonder if he even cares. There doesn't seem to be any way to tell. For me it is good to see my family again; they help relieve some of the tension.

My cousins depart around noon, leaving lots of assorted breakfast treats on the tray. Sam makes another pot of coffee. We sit and enjoy the leftovers and watch my father sleep. It is clear; our nervous and excessive talking has indeed worn him out.

The rest of the day passes much like the last two. Mary comes for her usual visit, staying for about an hour. Dad always perks up when he knows she's coming. I empty the contents of a new jigsaw puzzle onto the table and spend the afternoon sorting the pieces while listening to the two love-birds giggle in the corner of the living room.

Before heading back to Bill's, I receive a call from Elizabeth, a distant relative living in Santa Barbara. "I understand your father is seriously ill. I really want to pay my respects to him even though it's been a while since I've seen him." She continues her tale as my mouth drops open. "I have only weekends free because of my work, but I'll be arriving by Greyhound bus tomorrow at eight-thirty in the morning, traveling all night." I am too astounded to find the words to change her mind. Dad looks at me with a blank stare as I relay the phone conversation. It's been almost twenty years since they have seen each other. Neither of us has a clue why she's making this trip.

Dad and I concur; we just don't have the energy to entertain someone we rarely see. I assure Dad her visits with him will be short. "I'll take care of the situation for you. I'll find something to fill her time so you can rest."

I phone my friend Gloria in San Ramon, who has been very kind and supportive through this process, taking me out for short dinners once in a while. She knows the area and the scheduled events occurring each weekend. Once I put in a request for help, she comes to my rescue.

"I'll call your Dad's place around noon tomorrow. We'll agree on a meeting place, and I'll take you both to a huge flea market in Oakland. If I remember right, Elizabeth enjoys antiques and flea markets."

A flea market, I tell her, is a perfect solution to my problem.

Hooray, I knew my friend would take the ball from me for a couple of hours, that's just the kind of person she is.

Saturday, March 11th

Before the rest of the household begins to think about stirring on a Saturday morning, I quietly get ready to meet Elizabeth at the Greyhound bus station.

The bus pulls into its designated spot shortly after I park the car. Only three people emerge from its steel cocoon. Elizabeth looks very tired as she heads down the steps with an overnight bag thrown over one shoulder. Her long, brightly dyed red hair is in disarray. She's devoid of her usual makeup, and her body looks thin and frail. I am sure she hasn't eaten in a week. Riding most of the night in an uncomfortable bus, hearing the roar from the highway and the grinding of the motor probably was not conducive to much rest.

I take her to breakfast at a small family restaurant; one I know has very good food and is always packed on a Saturday morning. We have to wait for a table—*good; I was hoping that would be the case, more time to kill, less time at Dad's.*

Somehow, having this extra person here makes me feel exhausted. I am finding just smiling is an effort. It feels like I have to mentally pull the skin from my chin over my mouth to be able to make it stretch into a smile. I'm sure my face is falling off, slipping down my neck, resting in folds on my shoulders resembling a Basset Hound. Several times during our meal I glance at my compact mirror, positive I will see a marked difference in my appearance.

Too soon, our long, delicious breakfast is over and I can no longer prolong the inevitable. The drive from the restaurant to Dad's is fifteen minutes; it would be obvious if I further delayed her visit.

Sam greets us with freshly made coffee and I make the introductions. Elizabeth takes her cup into the living room where Dad is dozing. She drags a dining room chair opposite his recliner and begins to talk to him softly, asking him questions, trying to keep him alert.

"So how are you enjoying living in Hayward, Clarence?" "Have you made new friends?" And— "I hear you have a new lady friend, tell me about her," on, and on it goes. She seems to be doing very well. I don't think I could play this role with someone after such a long absence. It doesn't take more than an hour of continual conversation and I see Dad beginning to fade, looking to me for guidance and a way to escape.

"Oh, my, I forgot yesterday to go to Trader Joe's for Dad's soy milk. I also need to buy some other things in that shopping center. Elizabeth, how about you join me for a ride and let Dad take a nap?"

Ah, a chance to get out and breathe some fresh air. My face has still not begun to cooperate; my cheeks feel heavy, hanging below my chin. I work at forcing smiles in the appropriate places of our conversation.

After our trip to the store and another short visit with Dad, it is time to meet Gloria for a walk around the flea market. Gloria expertly carries on the conversation with Elizabeth while I stare glassy-eyed into a void.

On the drive back to Dad's I kill more time by stopping for Mexican take-out for dinner. Bill and Kathy are coming to help with the evening conversation and to be courteous to our newest visitor. Ordering enough food to feed the entire neighborhood, we wait at the bar. I gratefully down a couple of glasses of chilled Chardonnay and try to reacquaint myself with this lady.

Before I can put down our bundles of hot food, salad, rolls, and beverages on Dad's kitchen counter, Sam announces she has called hospice. "Mr. C has been running a fever most of the afternoon and the appearance of his incision disturbs me. Someone needs to look at it."

To validate her decision, she wants to show me the reason for her concern. Reluctantly I follow her into Dad's bedroom where he is resting. Sam pulls up his over-sized T-shirt. I have purposely not looked at his incision before. It nearly covers his entire abdomen! Good God, most of it is raw red with areas of gaping holes around the stitches. All I see while staring at Dad's stomach is the nightmare of death pouring out its putrid, smelly ooze. Dad's body is just too weak to bring forward the physical energy and nutrients to heal his wound. Our take-out spicy, Mexican dinner has lost all its previous appeal.

Bill and Kathy arrive and the five of us sit at the dining room table and eat the take-out food anyway, just to have something to do while we wait for word from hospice.

The call comes as we are finishing our meal; antibiotics will be delivered to the house in a couple of hours.

Tired, the four of us say goodnight to Sam and Dad, then head back to Bill's. Before we leave, Dad yells for me to come back to his bedroom. "After taking Elizabeth to the bus, would you go to church for me, to thank everyone for their kindness?" I assure him I will gladly go tomorrow.

Elizabeth naps in the car. Arriving at our 'motel,' I gather a fresh towel, washcloth, some clean sheets, a blanket, and blow up another air mattress, the one my brother loaned us when Joe was visiting. It is a good thing Bill and Kathy don't use this part of their home very often. It now looks more like a flophouse than a living room.

This long lost relative insists I set an alarm clock for 5:30 tomorrow morning. Her bus leaves for Santa Barbara at eight. "You know, Elizabeth, we're just 30 minutes from the station."

"But I want to make sure we get there an hour ahead of time so I get a good seat before all the other passengers arrive." It is eleven before we are finally settled for the night.

Sunday, March 12th

We groggily maneuver through our morning routines and hurry to the terminal. Greyhound stations are such ugly places to sit and wait in the morning hours. We are so early the heat has yet to be turned on. Most of the bulbs are missing in the overhead lights, and the only music comes from car radios blaring rap as they pass the station. The thud, thud, thud of the bass vibrates the walls of the building. Elizabeth and I sit together on a hard slatted wooden bench trying to stay warm with only our toes touching the cold cement floor. We are alone, except for the ticket handler behind her caged cubicle. I am too tired to talk. Instead, I open my book which I take with me everywhere I go, and begin reading. "What are you reading?" She asks. "Do you usually read that kind of book?" "Why did you choose that kind of book?" "Why do you like his writing?" She keeps jabbering at me. I answer her silly questions with only an occasional short sentence.

"*Damn it,*" *I want to shout, "Just shut up and leave me alone."* But I know she is trying to cope with something deep inside of her. For some unknown reason (to me and maybe to her), she has had to make this pilgrimage. I probably will never know the real questions she is pondering in her mind. But somehow, sitting here in this wretched place, that knowledge is not helpful.

The empty bus arrives on time. Its double doors swing open and Elizabeth steps up to the platform, and hands her ticket to the driver; the only person to go aboard.

Once she is settled and the doors close, I leave to attend the service at Dad's church. Dad has asked me to publicly thank the congregation for their continued support. Their cards and wonderful food are still pouring into his home. Driving into the church parking lot, I remind myself over and over: This task should be easy, this task *will* be easy. This hour will give me a rest from my other responsibilities.

As the service begins I let my mind wander.

In the early 1950's a large group of Episcopalians, of which we were members, decided to build a new parish closer to their homes. Land was purchased, and then a good-sized building which housed a declining tombstone business was located and purchased. Ground was broken before the empty structure was moved to the property. There's my father turning over the first shovel full of dirt, his picture was in the evening *Tribune*. Daddy was elected the first Warden, Mother was asked to play the organ and lead the choir. Most Saturdays we worked at the new site sprucing up the grounds and camouflaging the building's original purpose. Folding chairs were rented, a table was made for the altar, and the ladies sewed and embroidered the altar linens. Shrubbery and trees were planted, the building was painted. Daddy helped supervise; and as usual, was in charge. Wherever he has been, he has always taken an active part in his community. He continued the same pattern with this Unitarian church. He joined the Sunday school group, volunteered to set up chairs for Sunday services, and performed the duties of the 'official photographer.'

THAT'S JUST THE WAY LIFE IS...

Hearing the minister pray out loud for Dad jars me from my reverie. A small crack opens in the thick wall I have created to hold back my emotions. *"Tears are not going to begin, not now; I can't afford it. Don't cry, Leslie. Don't listen to the wonderful words being spoken. Silently sing a favorite John Denver song, tap your foot softly in rhythm—I can do this. Dad wants me here; I can complete this task."* I scream loudly inside my head. My efforts begin to work though the energy to seal the opened wound is more than I wanted to expend this morning. After the completion of the service I force a smile, shake hands, and thank everyone who asks after Dad.

Leaving the church, I scrutinize the neighborhoods leading to Dad's house. Broken down homes and cars, demolished articles littering the sidewalks, and grocery carts left on overgrown lawns litters the landscape. I am reminded of Oscar Wilde's children's story, *The Selfish Giant*. Spring didn't come to the Giant's yard because of his selfish attitude. Winter remained in his garden with barren trees and blizzard-like conditions until he showed kindness to others. It doesn't appear spring will ever be invited to this part of the county either. It is too ugly and dirty with teenage gangs roaming the streets or just 'hanging out' on someone's front porch. The paper reported last night a drunken 18 year old driving 90 miles an hour down a residential street near here, killed seven people. Dad is aware of all of the ugliness that surrounds his beautiful mobile home park. He deals with it. "That's just the way life is," he continually repeats to me and means every word of it.

* * *

A hospice nurse is with Dad when I arrive. She is checking on the incision and his grossly swollen, discolored feet and legs. "There is an infection in the incision and the antibiotics should clear it up." She cheerfully explains to all three of us. She tells us again why the ostomy bag has been positioned at Dad's waistline and that he will no longer be able to wear regular pants. I explain about the clothes I have ordered from a catalogue as Dad grumbles loudly,

"Well, by God, if I can't wear my slacks, I'll buy huge pants and wear suspenders then!" He smiles, visualizing how clown-like he will look.

How I will miss his wonderful spirit. The nurse pulls me aside as she heads for the door. "Don't be concerned about the areas of the incision that have not closed. In his condition, those areas will never close!" *Oh God! How much worse is it going to get?*

Arriving at my brother's condo later in the day I find the situation has gotten worse. Bill is having a real panic attack. Kathy is trying to calm him. I chime in; knowing neither one of us is really helping to resolve his hysteria. Bill works at home. Hired by real estate agents, he produces pen and ink and watercolor renderings of properties for sale. "My mind has been so preoccupied with Dad that I spent most of today painting the wrong property, then made irreversible errors on two other drawings—something I have never done before." So many people close to him have died of cancer in a very short period of time, he tells us, "I am reluctant to pick up the phone when it rings for fear it will be another friend or relative dying of this damn disease."

"Bill, I'm sorry," I softly groan.

He continues his ranting. "We might as well face life, we are all going to die of cancer. It is just a matter of time. Why, you might have it right now and not even know it." *(Yes, I think. I too might have it, but have not told anyone.)* "I might have it; we all might be infected. So many people are being diagnosed, it probably is contagious."

He downs more vitamins and pills meant to boost his immune system. I have never seen him so distraught. He acts and looks like an invisible monster is right behind him, pursuing him, watching his every move. This cancer monster is ready to pounce the first time he forgets to eat right, get enough sleep, or pop a vitamin.

I have to keep reminding myself that I really believe death is only going through God's door. That we go through this door each night when we sleep. The difference between sleep and death is simple. That when morning arrives we slip back into our bodies and wake up to a new day. In death we don't return. There are 13 million suns in our Milky Way. If each of those suns has a planet which supports life revolving around it, then we are only a 'goofball' in the universe. There is so much more happening right now than just my father dying. Please God; help me to see the bigger picture.

Monday, March 13th

This morning the sun is shining brightly, framed in a clear, deep blue sky. There is no hint of stormy weather. I open the living room windows next in my makeshift bedroom and feel the fresh, cool, spring air. It invites me to indulge in an early morning walk. Kathy has the day off from her hectic schedule, so we decide to steal some precious time before I head over to Dad's. We dig out our tennis shoes, spandex pants, and hooded sweatshirts. She knows a beautiful wooded area not far from here where we can walk a trail around a lake. Leaving the condo, I feel a little giddy, like playing hooky from a college class.

Lake Chabot is breathtaking. The trees have leafed out from their dormant winter state and a few branches hold the remnants of spring's blossoms. The smell of eucalyptus fills the air. Mallard ducks swim close to shore, hoping for a few breadcrumbs. The rhythm of our feet along the worn pathway begins a renewal process surging through our bodies. How I wish I had the time to enjoy the entire lake. I want to lose myself for days in the fresh smells of spring, listen to the sounds of the many birds attracting mates, and watch the squirrels swish their tails, chirping at one another. It is so peaceful and restful here. But we stroll for only an hour because I need to continue my drive to Hayward.

We stop at my now favorite coffee house for the usual low-fat muffin and latte. We sit on stools facing the sidewalk and watch the locals gulp coffees and read morning papers. Most people are regulars, greeting one another as they enter the shop. They look like they are continuing the routines they established years ago, not having to deal with a new crisis each day. I like to watch people doing normal, everyday activities. It helps to remind me that only my small part of the world is going crazy right now. Kathy and I hug, each going our separate ways.

Arriving at Dad's, I open the back door that leads into his laundry area, the same as I do each morning. I walk into the same scene I encountered yesterday. Have I walked onto the set of the movie, *Ground Hog Day*? Over and over, I experience the same characters performing the same activities. Dad is in the living room, dozing in his recliner. Sam is at the kitchen counter reading her worn, tattered Bible. Her little dog is curled up on a pillow in a far corner. The house is uncomfortably quiet. Sam greets me with a warm smile and a hug. Twice a day, with the help of his walker, he drags his body the length of his mobile home; once after breakfast to collapse into his recliner, then in the evening to reach his bedroom. I can feel his concentration with each step he takes.

Dad is noticeably weaker today. Despite this decline, his spirits seem amazingly upbeat. He is just a bit disorientated because of the heavy doses of morphine. His speech is often slurred and sentences are left unfinished. I remind him several times throughout the day, of the time and the day of the week.

Our hospice nurse checks in shortly after I arrive. She takes such good care of Daddy, listening to everything he has to say, treating him with the respect and dignity he deserves. She asks him to go back to his bedroom so she can better examine him. Today, as she listens with her stethoscope, she hears fluid in Dad's lungs. It's the cancer. Excusing herself, she goes into the kitchen, away from earshot, to call Dad's doctor. Because of Dad's irregular heartbeat and the detected fluid, the doctor suggests another medication to help the heart pump through the fluid. He also wants Dad to go to the hospital for more x-rays.

Why are they all trying to keep my father alive, for God's sake? "If medication is not given," the doctor continues on the phone, "he may die of a heart attack." *What a blessing that would be!*

The nurse checks Dad's incision and lets us know the oozing has let up some. That's one positive note. It looks like the antibiotics might be working. "However," the nurse continues, "there are parts of the wound which still have not closed." She asks me to come into his room to show me what she is talking about. *Why do I need to do this? Why does she want me to see this?* But part of my brain still seems to be functioning on a logical level. Perhaps she has to show me any new developments for insurance purposes, if for nothing else. I reluctantly lower my eyes to where she is pointing with her gloved finger; yet trying to avoid the horror of seeing deeply into his abdomen through his open wound.

Looking at her watch, she smiles and declares, "I'm sorry, but my time is up for now. Don't forget the x-rays." She bids us goodbye until the next time. I decide not to take Dad for x-rays tomorrow. He doesn't need to wait in the hallway of that department any more. "You know, Dad, the nurse hears fluid in your lungs, but I don't think you need to have an X-ray. It would be too difficult to get you to the hospital. I say we just skip it. What do you think?" He agrees with my decision and looks relieved to not exert any more energy. I don't tell him the cancer has spread to his lungs, just that fluid is now present. He is certainly no dummy; he knows what is going on with his body. I don't have to draw him a picture.

Sam empties Dad's two human waste bags, fixes him some lunch, and helps him into his recliner. These ugly chores completed, I feel comfortable enough to give Sam a break for the afternoon. He is lucid and pain free at the moment. I settle myself in Mother's chair and cradle his hand in mine. Occasionally we talk about my sons or my husband, the sunshine outside, and the shadows playing on the walkways. Time has halted; I can sense it all around us. Only the constant rotation of the anniversary clock's pendulum and its fifteen-minute chime remind us time *is* passing. He recalls fond memories with his boyhood buddies and reflects on the years with Mother. I like being here with my father right now. I am so grateful we have found this closeness. Quiet and peaceful times like these help me to cope with his cross words and obnoxious demands.

After a half hour of rest, Dad bursts out with an anger that appears to be swallowing him up almost as fast as his cancer. Only on rare moments when no one else is around, have I heard him complain about this whole ugly situation. Today is one of those moments.

He yells loudly, "Why didn't that damn doctor bother to discover the cancer in my leg months ago? I certainly brought it to his attention early enough. What's a-matter with the medical profession? I am being robbed of time with Mary, robbed of my life because of that one doctor. I have so much more I want to do and see." He quickly catches his breath and his words. His face hardens into a scowl, his lips tighten, his mouth barely moves, and he closes his eyes.

After sitting with him all afternoon through outrage, fond memories and dozing, I am overwhelmed with exhaustion again. *Can anyone comprehend what I am going through, I wonder? I don't even fully understand my own conflicting feelings.*

I recall making the mistake of trying to comfort Mother shortly after she was diagnosed with terminal cancer. Since she had only a few months to live, the doctor gave her an ultimatum. She could have extensive surgery that may prolong her life, though there was a strong possibility she might not survive the operation, or she could call hospice and remain comfortable at home for the duration. I watched her struggle with her decision.

"I know how you must feel, Mother," I innocently said to her with my hand on her arm.

"No, you don't!" she shouted. Scowling at me and stamping her foot, she blurted out in an authoritative and forceful voice, "You couldn't possibly know what I am feeling, and I pray to God you will never have to find out!"

She was right. I couldn't possibly know.

Sam returns in time to fix dinner for Dad. As I leave the mobile home park the left side of my chest erupts with pain. Can I be having a heart attack, I wonder? Or maybe it's the cancer I was told I might have in my left breast. I assure myself, all I need to do is to get to the condo, relax a bit. Take a few deep breaths. Have a glass of wine, open a good book. Then I will be okay.

* * *

The next couple of days blur together. A semblance of new routines begins to take form. At Dad's, I work on my jigsaw puzzle. Throughout the day people from his park, his home organ club, the Elks, and his church come to see him. They find my spread-out puzzle pieces on the dining room table a refuge. It gives his friends something to do while they pull themselves together and calm their nervous tension before going in to see Dad. Mary comes over every afternoon for a couple of hours. They sit and hold hands, chat, and giggle about nothing in particular.

Dad's incision still doesn't entirely close. It's not painful for him, just a bit ugly to look at. The nurse removed the staples and packed it with gauze soaked in a saline solution. Sam now has to change it twice a day along with her other chores. Dad is routinely eating smaller portions each mealtime. The hospice nurse tells us his red and grossly swollen legs and feet are due to cancer in his lymph system. Nothing can be done except to keep Dad as comfortable as possible. He knows the cancer is throughout his body. He knows it's only a matter of time. Will it be today?

"I'm tired of this old body," he says to me in a low whisper as we sit in the sunshine on his deck. "It certainly isn't doing me any good at this point! There's no longer any use in holding on to it." I nod my agreement. He turns to me, a small smile spreading across his lips. "I am ready for the next journey, just not in a hurry for it to begin. This day is too sunny and pretty."

In a lucid moment, Dad asks for a writing tablet and a pen to be within his reach at all times. He wants to write his own epitaph. He says he has it 'all up here' and points with his index finger to the right side of his head. "I'm working on it even when I sleep."

Wednesday, March 15th

Dear Gloria, my supportive friend, has invited me to her home for dinner tonight. Knowing I have an escape valve waiting, the day seems to glide by smoothly.

I arrive in the late afternoon after her day of teaching. We take a walk in the fading sunshine, return to her place, and sit around the kitchen table chatting, enjoying a freshly opened bottle of wine. Our conversation however, is constantly interrupted by what sounds like Gloria's infectious laughter coming from another room. This doesn't make sense. "Gloria, how can I be sitting across from you in the kitchen and yet I hear you laughing in another room?"

Ushering me into the living room she introduces me to her new parrot. The evening becomes hilarious. The parrot laughs uproariously every time his keeper's voice enters the conversation. I begin laughing uncontrollably. Tears run down my face, my sides ache, and still I howl. It feels so wonderful to laugh again. I spend most of the night giggling with my friend and her amazing, silly bird. *Laughter, what a healer! I had forgotten. She should rent out her parrot to geriatric wards and children's hospitals; no better medication could be prescribed.*

Thursday, March 16th

I feel sick to my stomach and a little dizzy this morning. Stepping into Jenny's bathroom to shower I notice a broken blood vessel in my left eye. My whole eye is blood red. I look like I was in a fight last night. Because of the swelling, it is also very uncomfortable when I blink. I stumble through my morning routines . . . routines are supposed to promote sanity. Wearing my dark glasses, I stop at the coffee shop on the way to Hayward for a quiet ten minutes, hoping to prepare myself for whatever awaits me.

Sam greets me at the back door with the information that Dad hasn't eaten this morning. He feels ill. He is bloated again, and is extremely uncomfortable.

We give him a Vicodin along with his morphine. I sit with Dad for the remainder of the day, holding his hand while he closes his eyes and tries to rest. All I can do is yawn. What a great pair we make, Dad emitting an occasional belch to relieve his discomfort while I sit next to him yawning! My right leg begins to throb. Now what? Whenever I get up out of the chair, I experience dizziness as well as pain again on the left side of my chest. Stress certainly has unique ways of expressing itself, and right now it is having quite a field day with me.

I leave Dad's house early in the evening. He is still uncomfortable and refusing to eat. I hurry back to Bill's. I've got to get to bed and escape with sleep. I am shaking with a deep, penetrating cold. I undress and curl up in a fetal position on my air mattress, tucking four blankets around me, hoping tomorrow I will be better able to function. Everyone tiptoes around me, trying to be quiet and respectful.

No matter what time we turn out our lights, no one in this house sleeps deeply anymore. Bill sleeps with the pager next to his bedside turned up to full volume. Kathy drags the phone to her side of the bed, trailing a long cord. We all anticipate the ring of the telephone or the buzz of the pager telling us there is a new crisis, to come quickly, Dad is nearing the end. We awake each morning feeling both disappointed and upset to have to be enrobed with another day of suffering yet, we are genuinely relieved that our father has more time.

Friday, March 17th

I am much better today, feeling able to meet the challenges waiting for me. The sky is a beautiful deep blue, no clouds anywhere as far as I can see. The sounds of spring are in the air. Most of Dad's neighbors have put up feeders attracting large groups of singing birds. Two doves are busily building their nest in one of the aluminum supports on Dad's deck. He says they have tried to build their home in that support every year. But time after time their efforts have been blown away by an afternoon wind. This year, Sam and I promise him, we are going to help this couple succeed.

With Sam's persuasion, Dad is eating a little today. Visitors parade in and out all morning long. Bill comes in the afternoon, something he is doing routinely now. We sit at the dining room table placing an occasional piece into the growing puzzle picture. Dad, who has been dozing for about twenty minutes after a stream of well-wishers, pushes himself up and out of his recliner, asking for his cane.

"I'm tired of sitting," he announces. "It's time to get out and walk." Startled, all three of us jump up. Sam hurriedly pushes his walker to him instead of his cane. Dad steadies himself and ambles to his office area, which we moved to the family room.

"It's time to get some work done and organize my desk! I need to pay bills and get my papers in order."

We watch him closely. We stay far enough away so as not to hinder his activity, but near enough to support him if he needs us. He displays the energy of a man half his age in excellent health! Busily opening every drawer, he goes through files, takes out papers and forms, signs where he is sure it is absolutely necessary, and throws away what he assumes to be trash. Only minutes after this spurt of energy begins, it dissolves with a cry to Sam. He needs a pill to be put under his tongue for nausea. With Sam's help, he manages to get back to his recliner and closes his eyes.

I remember hearing about this kind of behavior with terminally ill patients. It is similar to what a pregnant woman sometimes experiences before delivery, the *nesting instinct*. Without any warning, the mother-to-be has boundless energy. She sometimes rearranges furniture and involves herself in activities she hasn't attempted since the onset of pregnancy. Isn't death similar to a birth? Some births take a long, painful time; others are short, quick, and easy. Death is like that. The baby must go through a long dark tunnel to a new life. I am told the dying have similar experiences.

Saturday, March 18th

Dad's not doing very well today. He has excruciating pain in his stomach and feels nauseated. He takes Vicodin between the morphine doses. It makes him unable to concentrate; hence conversations become limited. I struggle to carefully maintain my fragile routine.

Watching him doze in his recliner, I look around the living room, down the hallway, and into his bedroom. His home seems to be falling apart at the same rate he is. The toilet was never fixed. We keep the lid off so we can flush it from inside the tank. The entire deck on the front of his house is rotting and needs to be replaced. Only yesterday I discovered a new leak under the house from the clothes washer. But crawling under houses and changing ostomy bags are two things I don't do! So we wait.

* * *

The retirement village is having a St. Patrick's dinner and dance at the clubhouse tonight. The Park has a social event every month for its residents and their guests. My optimistic father has purchased three tickets for this evening, one for Mary, one for himself, and one for me. By afternoon, he realizes he isn't going anywhere tonight. As always, he is concerned about the money he has spent. There is no refund on the tickets. Mary is uncomfortable going alone to this event. She knows she will be bombarded with questions from her neighbors as soon as she walks through the door. She wants me there for support. *My God, I sure don't want to go to a dumb celebration with old people I don't know!* I tell Dad of course I'll be happy to go and to accompany his lady.

He instructs me to call the president of the social club and ask him if we can use his third ticket to bring home a plate of food for Sam. "Oh sure," the president assures me, "just tell the caterers in the kitchen I said it was fine by me."

I have gone to a couple of these social affairs with Dad when he first moved into the village. They always seem like an excuse for the ladies to primp themselves, to wear one of their cocktail outfits left over from the 60's or 70's. So I need to dress better than I have the last couple of months, no frayed cotton pants and T-shirt.

Some of my clothes are still here at Dad's. I try on a couple of the dresses and two or three pantsuits. Nothing seems to work. They are either too tight or not appropriate. I opt for a pair of black slacks, with seams threatening to split around my hips. I add a long, silk blouse to further camouflage my problem.

I begin to work on my face. The circles under my eyes don't want to fade no matter how much concealer I use. My eyelids are so droopy I'm having trouble applying shadow correctly. What on earth is happening with this mirror? That can't be me in the reflection! If Mother were here she would say I look like 'something the cat dragged in!'

I work with different potions to make my face look like I am at least alive and well. I want to please Daddy and let him know I care for him. I need to wear a face that tells him I am looking forward to this event.

I drive the couple of blocks to pick up Mary so we can enter the entertainment hall together. Without exchanging a word, it is clear to both of us we wouldn't be going tonight if Dad hadn't insisted. We hold hands as we go inside, bolstering up the courage to spend the majority of the evening answering questions.

This is a BYOB party. We have all brought our drink of choice. I pour wine in a paper cup and drink it hungrily, hoping the pain of being here with all these people whom I don't know, and don't care to know, will somehow fade into the bottle and become invisible. Memories flood my consciousness, distracting my focus to happier times, remembering other parties.

> Part of Dad's job as superintendent of a large department store is to organize an annual party and dance. This year the party is held in the ballroom of Berkeley's famous Claremont Hotel. My date and I are invited to attend the festivities with Mom and Dad. Mother doesn't like going to big gatherings, so we are good company for her while Dad is checking on one or more of the details. I am also a great dancing partner for my father since Mother doesn't care to dance and dancing is Dad's middle name. My father can out dance me on any selection the band plays. He moves his feet in various configurations, showing everyone on the floor his mastery of the famous Balboa Hop from his high school days. The crowd cheers. Nothing slows down my father. It is his twenty-year-old daughter who has to continually go back to the table for a needed rest. The smile on his face is wide, his pinstripe suit is expertly pressed, and his shoes are polished to a mirror-like shine. His dark brown wavy hair lies perfectly in place, aided by his daily dab of Brylcreem. No beads of perspiration are detected on his brow. No labored breathing is heard after the band concludes its number. Dad just wants to know when will the music begin again!

The commotion of the dinner trays being placed on the center tables abruptly ends my daydreams. I go into the kitchen to get Sam a take-out plate of food ahead of the others. I pile on corned beef, cabbage, salad, and dessert before everyone gobbles it up. "This way," I tell the chef, "I will be able to get back here in time to go around the table for myself."

"Sorry", he says. "No one gets food before I say it's time and they certainly don't take it out of here."

"Look! This has already been cleared by the president of this affair," I answer back. "My father is sick and dying. He can't come here to get his own food. Now, if you would like to make up a plate and deliver it to him, fine. Otherwise I am helping myself."

"You can't do that!"

"Watch me!" I angrily shout back. *This place has rules for everything; and damned be the person who tries to bend them!*

Hearing the commotion, the president comes into the kitchen to investigate the racket. The chef's mouth falls open as he is told it's Clarence Compton who is dying at home. He knows Daddy, but like so many people, was unaware of his illness. "I didn't have any idea you were talking about Clarence. My goodness, take all you want, forget the tickets, take an extra plate for tomorrow."

My father leaves his mark wherever he goes.

I put the two heavily loaded paper plates in the car and drive back to Dad's. Pulling into the driveway, I am flooded with a sense of foreboding—*My God, Dad is worse!* Hearing me on the back steps, Sam opens the door. "Mr. C has begun vomiting. We have another emergency." Here we go again. I shove covered plates of food into the refrigerator . . . like other leftovers, they may never be touched. I walk into Dad's bedroom. He tells me he feels a blockage in his intestines just like before. He should know. It's his body, after all.

I call the 24-hour hospice number. The operator doesn't sound too happy about asking a nurse to come out on a Saturday night. "Due to illness in our department, we are operating on a skeleton crew." She takes a moment to look through Dad's chart. "I'm sure Mr. Compton is just constipated again, he'll be okay."

I'm not buying that one. "I insist you people do something, and fast. My father is in terrible pain." Hearing my tone of voice, she tells me someone will come out as soon as possible.

I drive recklessly back to the clubhouse, ignoring the speed bumps and 10-mile an hour signs. The residents have yet to be called to the buffet table. Everyone is obediently seated, drinking, talking, and waiting to be herded like sheep to the food troughs. Mary looks like she's having a good time after all. "Mary, I am so sorry, but Dad is in trouble again. We have called hospice and someone will be coming out. He's in terrible pain again. Can you find a ride home?"

"No problem, I'll find a ride. You just take care of Clarence." Good, that's one person I don't have to be concerned about. I have a feeling this may be another long night, so before I return to Dad's house, I grab some food for myself. Hearing grumbling in the background as I take a paper plate from the stack at the end of the buffet, I heap it with the freshly prepared St. Patrick's Feast and try to ignore the angry, hungry stares around me from people who are still waiting for their feast. *Screw them! Maybe they would like to take their dinner back to Dad's and help me tonight.*

Stuffing the food into Dad's refrigerator, I retreat to the living room where I sit and wait an eternity for a hospice nurse to knock on the door. Dad continues vomiting in the basin Sam holds for him. I can't go into his bedroom. I can't hold that basin. I can't stand the sound of his retching. I have never been able handle that sound. I also can't stand the overwhelming feeling of helplessness that has consumed me. And yet, I am jealous of Sam. She stands there smoothing my father's brow with a cool cloth and singing soothing hymns while he pukes in a bowl! Sam is an amazing person. I don't know how she does this all day long.

I try to drown out the cries of distress and pain and concentrate on the sounds of passing cars, hoping the next one I hear will stop in front of the house. I want to hear a car door open and close and the sound of footsteps clomping on the carpet-covered aluminum stairs. I want to hear the doorbell ring. I want to see a hospice nurse standing there. *Hurry, please hurry, we can't handle much more.*

We wait three hours while Dad continues his vomiting. The nurse finally arrives and gives my thoroughly worn out father the recommended laxatives and suppositories. She is sure, as was stated over the phone, Dad's problem is just constipation. *Damn it! This **isn't** a constipation problem.* But I don't say what is really on my mind. Instead I smile and generously thank the tired nurse for stopping by so late on this Saturday night.

At one AM, it looks like Dad may be settled for the night. Exhaustion has finally set in. I am not convinced that laxatives are going to solve his problem. At any rate, I kiss him goodbye and drive to Bill's for some badly needed rest. The streets are deathly dark and quiet at this late hour. Most sane people are snuggled under covers enjoying a good night's sleep. I silently enter the condo and strip off my clothes. I don't even bother to wash my face or to brush my teeth; I just need to rest. Sleep overtakes me even before my head hits the pillow.

The next thing I know Bill and Kathy are standing over me. They are fully dressed. I glance at my alarm clock; it is three-thirty in the morning.

"Sam just called us. Dad is being taken to the ER in an ambulance. We need to hurry so we can meet him there."

I quickly brush my teeth; I am concerned about having bad breath being around sick people. I throw on my discarded shirt and pants from the day before, and in five minutes we walk out the door.

We discover why the ambulance was called when we reach the hospital.

"I had just gotten to sleep after you'd left, when Mr. C yelled out to me in a panic-stricken voice. I ran into his bedroom to find the colostomy bag had separated from his body and had literally exploded from all the laxatives and suppositories."

"Oh my God, Sam."

"Fecal matter covered everything, and I mean everything. Once Mr. C was calmed down," *and I wonder how on earth anyone could become calm in a situation like this,* "I managed to get him into the shower, where he began retching again, this time vomiting fecal matter. I used twelve pairs of rubber gloves to clean him up."

She wrapped him in blankets and put him in his wheelchair, replaced his colostomy bag, redressed his incision, and then changed his bed. As soon as he was settled, she called hospice. They gave her permission to call 911, agreeing to pick up the tab. Then, she phoned us.

I can't even imagine what that experience was like for Sam or for my father. It is truly like a Steven King or Dean Koontz horror novel. This can't really be happening. This has to be someone's runaway imagination. *When can I awake from this horrible nightmare?*

All of us collapse into the all too familiar chairs in the emergency waiting room. The TV is still blaring in the corner, probably never turned off from the last time we were here. Mothers hold their crying children with ear infections. Heart attack victims recline on gurneys in the hall. An old lady is huddled in a wheelchair, her few strands of white hair sticking straight up. She pleads with the receptionist; "I'm out of pain medication and my insurance won't pay for more. Please, just one more bottle. Please." We wait with the others in silence.

Dad is a priority because he arrived in an ambulance and is seen quickly. The doctor sends him to X-ray. No new blockage is detected. The doctor tells us the only option now is to insert a tube down Dad's throat to ensure that nothing, not even saliva, reaches his stomach. The tube will remain until death. We can't face this right now; we are all on overload.

"Sorry, Doctor", I want to say, "no decisions can be made right now. We can't handle any more bad news, we are crammed full tonight. We'll have to rewind that last conversation and try it again."

A second physician is called in. He decides we don't have to be so hasty after all.

"Let's do a little experimenting here," he says. "Let's just see if Mr. Compton can keep down liquids. If he can keep fluids down, we won't have to insert that tube." Dad begins to tentatively sip water with a straw, sucking slowly, afraid of the end result.

Again we sit and wait. We try to fold our bodies to be small enough to steal a few minutes of sleep in the hard green plastic chairs. We take turns visiting our father. His spirits remain high as he continues to joke with the 'pretty' nurses.

Kathy seems to be the only one with her head still screwed on right. She goes to her car and returns with a stack of the latest magazines she quickly gathered from her house before our hasty departure.

It is six in the morning. We are rummy and hungry. Sleep will be out of the question for the remainder of the day. Kathy slips out again, this time returning 20 minutes later. "There's coffee, bagels, and muffins in my car," she announces, and then suggests we take turns retreating for a much-needed break.

I smell the delicious aroma of freshly brewed coffee and warm gooey sweet rolls when it's my turn to escape. Nestled in the bag are also several kinds of bagels and a variety of cream cheeses. Paper plates, napkins, and plastic knives are carefully placed in the back seat for each shift. What a sweetheart! I sip my hot caffeine drink, eat a yummy cinnamon roll, and listen to the hum of the early morning traffic outside the parking lot. In the solitude of the car, I take a long deep breath, acutely aware of all the wonderful supportive people enveloping me. Thank you. My father and I are truly fortunate. But all too quickly I have to return to the din of the fast-paced emergency room.

By eight, we learn Dad can return home. He is to remain on liquids for the rest of his days. He rides back to his house in an ambulance, the same way he left only hours before. We are all blurry-eyed and dog-tired. Father is put to bed to rest. Bill stretches out on the living room floor. Kathy takes a blanket to the deck, plops down on the chaise lounge, and quickly closes her eyes. I sprawl out on the ugly green sofa Mother occupied during her short bout with cancer. We nap, knowing that in a couple of hours a hospice nurse will arrive. And later in the day, Dad's minister is expected. But right now this short respite feels very, very welcome.

With only two hours' rest, Kathy has to leave for work. Bill goes with her. I am alone again.

Our favorite hospice nurse arrives. After her visit with Dad, she orders an oxygen tank to help him breathe easier during the night. We have our usual conversation out of his earshot next to her car.

"We talked about your father at our meeting this morning. No one was surprised with the problem he experienced last night. They just hadn't expected it to show its ugly face this soon. You need to be aware this last crisis could be repeated anytime. When it happens again, there will be nothing we can do except to let him continue vomiting until his body finally gives out."

"Oh my God," I whisper, tears pooling in my eyes. But she is not through. As much as I would like her to leave, she continues with further bad news.

"Your father's incision is infected again. The wound is enlarging every day. I am not recommending antibiotics this time. Our hope is to have the infection take over his body so he can have a soft death."

As the nurse climbs into her car and drives away, I feel the tension building again. My chest and gut feel like a two-ton cinder block has been added to my already overburdened load. I don't want my father to go through this experience again. **I don't want to go through this nightmare again.** *How much more can we take, Lord?*

I trudge up the front stairs feeling like I should be the one to have an oxygen tank just to reach the last and third step leading to the front door.

Dad continues to rest on his circulating airbed. The motor hums softly throughout the house; it is the only sound in what feels like a deathly quiet aluminum tin can. I listen for changes in Dad's breathing pattern and hear none. I now know that any minute, any second, things could go downhill. I tiptoe to Dad's computer, careful not to wake him, determined to give myself just a few more minutes of peace.

I email Joe. I ask him to write a letter to our friends requesting prayers for Dad's quick demise and prayers for strength to continue with my part in this process. I know I must go through this agony with Dad. I don't want anyone to take this from me, only God, please give me the strength and courage to go down this ugly road so he will not be alone.

I stumble through the next couple of days, staggering through the routines I have set for myself, trying to stay awake while driving to and from Dad's house. Each day, Sam gets him out of bed, bathes him, and gives him a shave. She shuffles him to the sink to brush his teeth and dresses him in the over-sized T-shirt and the loosely cinched drawstring flannel pants that have finally arrived. She places him in his wheelchair, for he no longer has the strength to use the walker. She then pushes him to the kitchen table to eat his breakfast of Jell-O, cran-rasberry juice, and hot tea. Afterwards she wheels him to his reclining chair in the living room, where he remains for the rest of the day. With a urine bag and a colostomy bag, he doesn't even have to get up to go to the bathroom . . . a small blessing.

For lunch he is given multiple medications and a fruit 'smoothie' made with Boost (a vitamin-enriched drink) or a taste of mashed potatoes. He sleeps in his chair, answers the phone, reads his mail, and watches the weather report three times a day. Dinner is presented with more Jell-O, broth, and fruit juice.

Wednesday, March 22

I enter the house as usual and find Dad sitting in his recliner, smiling and talking on the phone.

"I've had a very good week. With a couple more weeks like this, I'll get some of my energy back and be on my feet again."

Seeing I have arrived, he hangs up the phone. "Leslie, will you get me the church hymnal from the bookcase? I want to pick out the hymns for my memorial service." *These ups and downs are terrible. I never know from minute to minute what to expect.*

While Dad thumbs through the hymnal, I attend to the tasks of keeping this household running. I call PG&E. Because of the oxygen and airbed Dad is using, hospice told me we could get a discount on our electric bill. The utility company informs me this can't be handled over the phone. In order to obtain the discount, I will have to drive to San Leandro and fill out the forms. At least this trip gives me a break in my day. But Dad will probably be dead before the paperwork goes through their system.

Later in the day I turn on Dad's computer. The flood of emails is astounding. Once again, I am reminded, I am not alone:

"You are being held in my thoughts and prayers daily. I really admire you for being there for both of your parents when they needed you the most."

"You and your family are in our prayers. This is the most dreadful thing to go through. I know the disruption in your lives is very difficult, if you need a shoulder please feel free to call or write. We love you."

"I have no words to console you except to say that you continue to be in my prayers. I pray that the Lord will strengthen you, your dad, and all those around you who continue to care for your dad. May you be comforted by the knowledge that God is always there."

"Dearest, we're sending you our love, big, warm hugs, and all the support you can grab hold of over these Internet lines. Just imagine that global mind *is* reality and that even though you are far in miles, we are right there with you in our consciousness. It seems the whole world is spinning beyond even our fantasies of control. I guess treading water is about all we can hope to accomplish. And maybe that's all we really do anyway—we just think we're getting all these great things accomplished."And--

"Our prayers are with Pappy and with you. Your father is a wonderful man and is very lucky to have you as a daughter. We are praying that he will have peace and comfort in his final days. I can't begin to understand what you are going through. We pray that God gives you the strength you need. We will be here for you when you come home."

Sometimes it takes a crisis to realize how much we are cared for and loved. Silently, I offer a thank you to everyone. I am very blessed.

Sunday, March 26th

There was no phone call last night, no blast from Bill's pager, but I wake up tired anyway. I move through my routines in slow motion, taking my time to get ready to go to Dad's this morning. While brushing my teeth, I suddenly remember today is my wedding anniversary. Next year, I tell the face in the mirror, I am going to have a huge celebration on the twenty-sixth of March; I am not doing this one again!

* * *

Dad appears to be feeling fine this morning, or as fine as he can feel under the circumstances. As soon as I open the door he informs me that he expects Sam and me to take him to the clubhouse after lunch. An organ concert will be given there next Sunday. The guest organist is coming this afternoon to practice. On center stage in the clubhouse is Mother's huge three-manual home organ that Dad donated after she died. Dad is still the president of the Home Organ Club. He feels an obligation to be there to meet the musician.

"I must tell this man about the idiosyncrasies of that instrument," he insists. "It must be played correctly to emit its fullest sound and I am the only one who can instruct him."

"Okay," we tell him, knowing this will be a tremendous challenge for all of us. "We will do our best to get you to the clubhouse."

Helping him dress, I notice blood has begun to pool in the backs of his feet as well as his spine. That his body is shutting down doesn't seem to deter his efforts right now. He must go to the clubhouse, that is what he needs to do, and he needs to do it, 'right now.'

Sam and I calculate the timing. Getting Dad into his wheelchair, out of the house, out of the wheelchair, down his steps, into the wheelchair, then to the car, into the car; drive the short distance, then out of the car, set him in the wheelchair, and into the clubhouse. We figure it will take us a good half hour to go the four blocks. Thank God it's not raining!

Dad brushes his hair again and applies his aftershave. I put slippers on his swollen red feet. His shoes no longer fit. Together Sam and I gingerly lift him into his wheelchair and begin our carefully rehearsed four-block trek.

Dad meets the organist and doles out instructions about the workings of this precious instrument. It is clear, through his comments and facial expressions; the musician already knows much of what Dad has to say. Finally, Dad, realizing he is no longer in charge, throws up his hands and looks towards the ground.

"Okay, okay," he says with a resigned smile. "I just wanted to make sure there were no questions about next Sunday in case I don't make it."

This short encounter leaves Dad exhausted and anxious to head home. It has taken a toll on Sam and me as well, making the return trip home even more difficult to orchestrate.

In the evening I return to my safe harbor. Bill is pacing and ranting loudly in the living room.

"I've fucking had it! I can't take this fucking roller coaster anymore. I'm not going to deal with it. I have nothing more to say to Dad except ask him about the weather. When I come to see him tomorrow, I'll smile, wave to him, ask him about the weather, and then go to the dining room and put in some more puzzle pieces on your damn puzzle, Leslie."

We talk. We shout. We yell. We scream. We hug and hold each another. We are grateful to be together. We swear vulgar obscenities and call Dad ugly names, laughing as we do so. We cry and embrace. This journey is so difficult. All of us are out of reserve energy. We operate only from pure nerves. One day Dad is on his way out. Sure to die by morning. The next day, he rallies. How much longer can he hang on?

Monday, March 27th

I can almost see Dad's body separating from his spirit. His head remains clear. He continually directs us to complete the tasks he feels are absolutely necessary. And accomplish them we must—immediately! Dad conducts this show from his recliner, ordering whoever is within earshot to bring him items he wants worked on. It is as though he has left his poor sick body in his bedroom so he can continue to function in the living room. I am convinced, even after Dad's body gives out, he will still be barking orders and placing phone calls.

* * *

I wish I could sneak into Dad's house undetected. Today, Dad is perched in his wheelchair, sitting on the deck enjoying the fresh air filled with the aroma of spring flowers. But he appears to be agitated. He has a pad and pencil in his lap. Seeing me, he begins to talk about a garden. Amazingly he still has some energy after his exhausting trip to the clubhouse yesterday. Since moving to this house he has planted a vegetable garden religiously every spring.

"It is getting too late in the year to plant, we have fallen behind," he exclaims. He wants me to buy six different tomato plants, string beans, three zucchini squash, lemon cucumbers, green peppers, and yellow squash. *Where will I get the energy to plant a garden?* "Don't forget," he continues, "lots of fertilizer must be worked into the clay soil before you plant the vegetables so they will thrive. And the only fertilizer acceptable is chicken manure." *I prefer to call it chicken shit; it just feels better.* "You mustn't delay a minute longer!"

Sam and I look at each other with blank stares. Did we both just hear the same demands? I can't believe he wants a garden planted right now. He won't even be around when the fruits of our labor finally mature! In fact, it is unlikely that any of us will be here in this house when the vegetables are ready to be picked. God, I hope not.

He has drawn the plot for his garden labeling the vegetables with X's, for he is unable to write the words.

"I want the tomatoes here where I have written in tomato." *He doesn't realize there are no words on his garden plot, only X's.* Moving his pencil over the pad of paper in his lap, he continues in his demanding voice.

"Over here you must plant the beans. You have to get rid of some of last year's tomato runners; they keep popping up all over. Now over here you plant the lemon cucumbers. Sam has never had a lemon cucumber, so I want to make sure she can try some of mine."

And on and on. Dad tries to control everything around him in an uncontrollable situation. I pretend I can read words into his X marks and go along with his demands. I continue to humor him. There is no way to argue rationally. I promise Dad that tomorrow morning I will stop and buy the necessary items to begin his garden.

I email my husband to send my old work clothes in an over-night package so I can dig in the soil.

After about 45 minutes of garden instructions, Dad seems satisfied that his wishes will be carried through. He is worn out and asks to be put into his recliner for a nap. I am sure he is spent for the day, so I retreat to my puzzle. I luxuriate, letting my mind wander, remembering another garden a lifetime ago. It is so much easier to concentrate on pleasurable experiences of the past than to be here in the present.

> I was expecting our first son in the unbearably hot summer of 1974. We had recently moved into our first home, a real fixer-upper. No problem with repairs and makeovers. Dad had just retired, and was happy to come to our rescue. After surveying the needed improvements, the equipment and time necessary to implement those improvements, he delighted in discovering a large plot of land along the side of our house. "Aaahhh," he exclaimed, "there is enough land here for a large, beautiful vegetable garden." He loved to garden, but it was too shady to grow vegetables in his own yard in Orinda.
>
> One of my fourth grade students lived on a show-horse breeding ranch. They let us truck several loads of the exclusive five-year-old manure to our plot of land. Dad felt I had located gold! A real treasure.
>
> Every morning around seven, the whistle of our teakettle would awaken me. That was my signal; Dad was there. He had used his own key, let himself in, and put the kettle on for Folger's instant coffee.
>
> Taking his cup of hot java out to the front porch, he would join Joe. A smile always spread across my face as I watched

those two through the breakfast window. There they were, every day that summer, working side-by-side, creating a lovely home for us. They built a double garage, redirected the driveway, landscaped the front yard, and of course spent time nurturing Dad's prized vegetable garden.

Our garden's bounty was soon larger than any other in our area. It was that seasoned manure and the special love and care Dad was willing to give to his adored leafy vegetables! He did forget however, that one needs only a couple of zucchini plants in a garden; ten really was a bit much, even when I shared with the neighborhood. I spent the rest of my summer learning to create recipes for the zucchini; breaded, stuffed, baked, fried, barbecued, as well as a special zucchini bread that received a blue ribbon at the state fair.

The scorching heat never slowed them down. Each afternoon I made lemonade, iced tea, and prepared humongous sandwiches to give them a break in the 90-100 degree heat. I can still see the sweat glistening on their bodies and their drenched shirts clinging to their backs. Periodically, they removed their baseball hats and wiped the perspiration from their foreheads with the backs of their hands to avoid the salty water flowing down their faces and stinging their eyes.

That summer Dad taught Joe everything he would ever need to know about repairs and construction. They cemented their relationship, developing a close bond that has lasted a lifetime.

I'd like to have just one day from that summer, just one hour to hold in my heart again. I can still see this trim, fit, 60 year old wearing fashionable bushy gray sideburns, jeans, and a plaid short-sleeve shirt. I can hear him loudly issuing instructions to Joe and then retracting his tone of voice to add softly, "Hey, anything you say, Joe, you're the boss." A wonderful summer ... full of hope, promises, and new growth.

Tuesday, March 28th

It is 68 degrees on this beautiful, sunny, spring morning. A wonderful day to hike in a State park, surrounded by towering redwoods and cedars, or to walk barefoot on the wet sands of the Pacific beach listening to the pounding of the surf, or to stroll along an inland lake watching the ducks tend their fuzzy, young chicks. Anything, anywhere . . . but being stuck here inside this hot, stuffy mobile home.

Today, Dad has called a meeting of the executive board of the Home Organ Club. He plans to formally hand over his office as president. He is not leaving this life until he is able to put closure on all his obligations. He wants reassurance that the organizations and activities where he was an active member continue after he is gone.

I have purchased cookies at a nearby bakery and Sam has set up her special coffee maker. I straighten the furniture and drag dining room chairs into a semi-circle around Dad's recliner in the living room. I can't believe my father in his condition, is actually going through with this meeting.

Dad is ready for his fellow board members. He has a note pad and a pencil on his lap. Next to his chair he has an organized file folder holding minutes from past meetings and phone numbers of all the members. He checks a hand mirror to make sure I have combed his hair properly. He wants to look presentable to his friends. His swollen feet, elevated in his recliner, have been shoved into slippers, trying to hide the pooled blood.

I greet each guest at the door with a smile and serve coffee and cookies as they gather around their leader. Dad calls the meeting to order. I back out of the way and into the kitchen, to be within earshot but not to intrude. The members are quick to jump in and help him when he falters with words or forgets what he is saying. When he begins to doze someone calls out his name or asks him a question. They want to make this meeting appear as normal as possible. They joke and talk in between business items while munching on their treats. They seem glad for the diversion of food to stuff down their overwhelming emotions. These people have known and worked with Dad for ten, fifteen years. I wish they would hurry up with their chitchat and all go home. I can see Dad quickly tiring. But he feels he must continue until all the business has been completed.

After two hours of chatter, the board members stand up and leave as a unit. The meeting is finally over. I'm anxious to get Dad settled for a badly needed nap.

Instead of closing his eyes to rest, he becomes very agitated. Suddenly he declares in a loud, aggressive tone, "I have to find the invitation we created for your mother's memorial service!" He rummages through what drawers and shelves he can reach without leaving his recliner.

"I'll look for it, Dad. Bill and I have copies if we can't find one here. I'll bring one over tomorrow."

"No, I want to find it now. I have got to make up my own invitation and I want to use Mom's as an example," he continues to shout.

"I *will* find the invitation." I am finally able to reassure him. "Dad, just give me a little time to go through your drawers and cabinets."

He collapses and closes his eyes. I search through the rest of the shelves and bookcases in the living room, the dining room, and the family room, and locate a creased invitation in the bottom drawer of his desk. Pulling it out to review, I stop for a moment to remember. Dominating the front page is Mother seated at her electric organ wearing an exuberant smile, ready to play a piece for the Oregon club.

Later I ask, "What pictures do you want for your invitation, Dad?"

We reminisce about favorite photos from years past. He chooses the one he thinks will best represent his life. Unfortunately that picture is in Boston. I took that photograph years ago of Dad at the beach with his big camera on a tripod and had it enlarged to a poster for his birthday. It looks like another over-night package for Joe to pull together.

Dad continues to discuss his memorial service, the songs to be sung and the celebration afterwards. I take notes. "I want a luncheon held here at the clubhouse."

"Okay, let's use the caterer we arranged for Mom's service a couple of years ago. I thought they did a terrific job." He informs me he was not fond of their food. *Funny, he sure ate enough, as well as the leftovers.*

"But Dad, I had the same people cater your 60th wedding anniversary. You said they did a great job."

"Yeah, but I didn't think the food was very tasty. I don't want them to do the catering. You must call the people who always cook the food for our special affairs at the clubhouse. They are the only ones to put on my luncheon. I want the whole park invited; a big party with music. And don't forget to put a map on the back of the invitation for all the people who don't live here."

A party for all the residents? My God, does he realize how much that will cost? Everyone will show up just for the free food, even if they have no connection with Dad. Mr. Compton who? Did he die? So sorry. Oh, well, where are the eats?

Dad is insistent about everything this afternoon. He wants closure immediately. Throughout our conversation he continually interjects with reminders about the Neptune Society. He wants to be sure that I can locate their phone number instantly. He and Mother signed up and paid for their cremation years ago. He wants to be in charge of his death as he has been in charge of his life. I feel like telling him I am going to program the Neptune's phone number into his damn telephone. I know he will want to make those final arrangements himself. As soon as I see him take his last breath I will put the phone in his hand and let him push the button the split second before he dies! *Why the hell doesn't he give it up?*

He begins to complain about feeling nauseous, I am not surprised. I can see by his green complexion and dark sunken eyes that he has overexerted himself. I know I have. But he manages to push himself one last time. Mary will be arriving very soon. He rests. He tries to pull together the last threads of strength and energy for his sweetheart.

Shortly after she arrives it becomes evident the eagerly anticipated visit is not going well. Dad is just too exhausted. I can hear snippets of their conversation as I sit at the dining room table locating pieces to complete my puzzle.

"I can feel each day I am getting weaker and weaker. I want to die as my wife did. She just shut her eyes and went into a coma. I am ready to go." He smiles up at her. "But I would like to stay here just a little longer."

Suddenly his body lets him know it won't take any further abuse. Dad begins vomiting. Sam helps him into his wheelchair and pushes him into his bedroom. Mary follows, carrying the basin. Remaining in the dining room, but within earshot of the loud, ugly retching sounds, I sit paralyzed. He doesn't need me back there. Sam and his lady are enough. I couldn't do anything anyway. I'm sure Mary wishes she had called with an excuse not to come today.

Has the time arrived that our hospice nurse warned me about? Will he continue vomiting until he finally checks out?

After about twenty minutes, Dad leans back onto his pillow and closes his eyes. The emergency seems to have passed, at least for the moment. Mary quietly slips out the back door, without even a wave or a nod to me. Sam settles into the warmed chair Mary has vacated and pulls it closer to Dad's bed. She remains with him holding his hand until she is sure the crisis is over. I stand hesitantly in the doorway. Dad's breathing becomes quieter, rhythmical. I step into his bedroom; Sam puts her finger to her lips as if to say "quiet, do not disturb Mr. C." If I didn't see the rise and fall of Dad's chest I would say he was dead. He wears the color of death. I want to go now. He doesn't much resemble the man I knew only a few short months ago.

APRIL

The Zest of Life

Let me but live from year to year,
With forward face and unreluctant soul.
Not hastening to, nor turning from the goal;
Not mourning for the things that disappear
In the dim past, nor holding back in fear
From what the future veils; but with a whole
And happy heart, that pays its toll
To youth and age, and travels on with cheer.
So let the way wind up the hill or down,
Through rough or smooth, the journey will be joy;
Still seeking what I sought when but a boy,
New friendship, high adventure, and a crown,
I shall grow old, but never lose life's zest,
Because the road's last turn will be the best.

—Henry Van Dyke
*(From Mother's college collection
of her favorite poems)*

Saturday, April 1st

I have trouble writing to my friends, I can no longer talk to anyone about Dad or what we are going through. I ask my husband to periodically email everyone with updates. They understand why I don't write any longer and instead send me wonderful letters.

"Dear Leslie,

I am writing to offer my assistance, prayers, and hopes for your father's gentle passing into the next life. I cried when I read what your poor dad had to experience. Why he was chosen to endure such trials is a puzzle, but I know that our Lord has a plan for each and every one of us. I also pray for you and your brother that you have the strength to continue through this ordeal and that you find some bright spot each day to help you through these difficult times."

* * *

The weather is beautiful and spring-like again this morning. But Dad has very little energy to enjoy the sunshine. He is extremely upset. He weighed himself as soon as he got out of bed. "I have lost fifteen pounds! I'm going to begin eating five meals a day from now on," he yells to me when I come through the back door. "I need to regain those lost pounds so I can get back some of my energy."

Dad still badgers us with his insistent commands. Because each day he is able to do less, he demands more from us. I know from reading the hospice booklet, this agitation is one of the markers of the beginning of the steep decline. It is almost a burst of energy in the form of panic as unconsciously Dad recognizes he is on his way out.

Sam takes direction from Dad always with a smile. "Okay, Mr. C, I'll be right there," she calls out to him. At least I get to leave this place each evening. I ask her how she is able to handle Dad's outbursts. "This is very common in terminally ill patients," she answers. "I'm used to this kind of behavior." She also tells me in the same breath that it's not unusual to have to restrain patients at this time because they become too belligerent.

Oh God, I hope we won't have to go down that road.

Sunday, April 2nd

I take a longer time to get ready to drive to Dad's this morning. He has requested that Sam and I take him to church. He says this will probably be the last time he can attend a service other than his own. No matter how hard I try, I just can't get enthusiastic about dressing up. I know I need to wear something other than the worn Levis and golf shirts I have so carelessly thrown on my body each morning. I finally decide on a simple jeans skirt, blouse, nylons and flat shoes. Anyway, my hair is clean, does that count?

Everyone in Bill's household is going somewhere different today. We are having difficulty getting organized all at the same time. I am getting myself into a tizzy. I know how upset Dad will be if I am the least bit tardy.

I drive through Hayward faster than the allotted speed limit, searching behind stop signs, around corners, and parking lots for that inevitable cop car waiting to nab me. As I turn into Dad's driveway, I realize I am ten minutes later than the time we agreed on last night. *Hold your breath, Leslie. Here comes the onslaught of verbal abuse.* I am not disappointed. As soon as I open his back door, Dad lets out with his tirade.

"Where have you been all this time? We have to hurry now to get to church on time. Last night I told you when to be here, weren't you listening?"

I know no explanation will be good enough.

Sam comes out of the guest bedroom greeting me with a beaming smile. She looks lovely in a tea-length black dress, black nylons, and black suede heels. I haven't seen her in anything but hospital greens for weeks. I forgot she was an attractive woman. Dad, of course, is all dressed up in his flannel drawstring pajamas, bedroom slippers, and a freshly pressed shirt. His hair is combed; he is cleanly shaved, and smelling of Mary's favorite aftershave.

I move the car to the front entrance. Sam and I help Dad down the stairs, into his wheelchair, and push him the four feet to the car. Life is good. We are going to church and the weather is beautiful.

We arrive fifteen minutes before the service. Because of our handicap sticker, I am able to park the car right next to the front door. "See, Dad? No problem with the time, not when I am in charge!" The minister greets everyone at the door as she does each Sunday. She gives Dad a warm, comforting hug.

Dad wants to sit in the middle of the congregation. That's easy enough to do; it is just a matter of moving some of the folding chairs to finagle his wheelchair into the center of the room. Sam and I arrange our chairs on either side of him. He tenderly holds her hand and she periodically gives him a warm, loving smile. *Hey! I'm here too, on the other side of you, Dad. I see myself sitting in this uncomfortable chair next to a sick man in a wheelchair.* But I don't feel like he has any knowledge of my being anywhere near him. Oh, well, I guess my position in this family has been demoted to just a taxi driver. What next, garbage collector?

During the service, Dad helps Sam locate the hymns and responses in the hymnal, which has been placed on everyone's chair. This Sunday there is no mention of Jesus in the service; not even any mention of God, this is a Unitarian Church. "Love is the spirit of this church," we all recite, "and service its law. This is our great covenant: to dwell together in peace, to seek the truth in love, and to help one another." It sounds good to me, what better way to live?

In the middle of a Unitarian service members of the congregation come forward, light a candle, and express their joys or sorrows. When all the candles have been lit there is a moment of silence to give thanks and to pray for those who are in need. Dad is unable to come to the front of the church to light his candle; he raises his hand to speak out.

"I want everyone to meet an angel. This person on my right—stand up, Sam," he whispers. "This is Sam. Without her I would be dead today. She is truly a blessing and I am very thankful she has come into my life. I want to light a candle for my many blessings."

The minister lights a candle and offers a special prayer for Dad and Sam. Tears unexpectedly flood my eyes. What a gallant gesture on his part. What an amazing man, my father. This is the reason he was so insistent on coming to church today. At the same time I am upset at myself. I'm jealous . . . really jealous! *Who is this Sam who can just walk into our lives and take over? Where are my 'goodies' from Dad?* Why didn't he also say, "I came to church today because I want everyone to know how thankful I am to have such a loving and caring daughter." I haven't heard that statement declared.

Why am I always the one to receive his sharp tongue and disapproving frowns while others receive his smiles? In spite of being reassured by hospice that the dying sometimes make the most impossible demands on those they love, I find this *normal behavior* is sometimes impossible to handle. I sit silently. There are too many emotions for me to think about lately. I'll deal with them later. They will just cloud over what is really important: Dad's peace of mind and physical well-being.

People come to Dad after the service, no longer asking him how he feels, no longer lingering with small talk, just, "It is so good to see you again, Clarence." "Nice to meet you, Sam." And on and on they chatter. I can see Dad is tired; this has been an exhausting morning. We need to get him home.

He is very uncomfortable on the ride home. The morphine is not eliminating his pain. I drive up to his front entrance, open the trunk, lift out his folded wheelchair, and push the lid closed. Sam and I lift him into the chair, wheel him four feet to the steps, lock the chair, help him out, and support him on each side so he can take one stair at a time to his front door. After each step he has to rest for a moment before rousting enough energy to climb the next hurdle. As he puts his feet on the landing, I run back down the stairs to the sidewalk, grab the wheelchair, and haul it up to the porch. I unfold it and place Dad back into the sagging vinyl seat. He heaves a deep sigh, knowing he doesn't have to move anymore. We wheel him into his living room. He asks us to just leave him. He is too weak to get into his recliner. Sam goes into her bedroom and changes into her comfortable 'greens,' the clothes Dad can spit up on and not ruin.

I'm so tired. Why does something like this just wear me out? I'm not the one who is sick, am I? But that question won't be answered until I get back to Boston. After half an hour of rest, Dad lets us help him into his chair where he can be more comfortable. My puzzle, my glorious jigsaw puzzle is just about complete. I can zone out again as Dad sleeps.

It is deathly quiet in here. I concentrate on the singing birds outside. The outside temperature is warming up, so I open the windows for a refreshing scent of spring air. I hear bits of conversations as walkers meander in the front of Dad's coach. I notice the two doves have been successful with their nest building. Sam has done some miraculous reinforcing. There are three little eggs nestled in the twigs, twine, hair, and down. They will be able to raise a family after all.

Monday, April 3rd

Yesterday was too much for Dad. He remains in bed, connected to the oxygen tank, and is unable to keep any food down. Even sips of water are not settling well. The outside temperature has risen to 80 degrees as predicted; the comfort zone of Dad's home is now a thing of the past. Dad's bedroom is hotter than the rest of the house. Both the oxygen and the mattress motors pump hot air. The afternoon sun floods his room. I tack up old sheets to deflect the light on the west windows. In the tool shed I locate the over-sized forty-year-old floor fan the folks used in Orinda and set it up in his bedroom.

Sam and I alternate shifts sitting by Dad's bedside. When it is my turn I bring a book to read. I touch his hand or brow every few minutes to remind him he is not alone. His eyes remain closed. The only sounds are the flow of air hissing from the inflatable bed and the oxygen tank assisting Dad's irregular breathing.

My friend Gloria rescues me again and invites me for an early dinner. Driving from Dad's house, we see a man running toward traffic on the other side of the street. He is frantically waving his hands and yelling for help. Blood is dripping from his head, covering his face and the front of his shirt. I can't believe the emergencies and catastrophes that keep entering my life. I dial 911 with my Massachusetts cell phone and listen to the different tones and signals as it locates Hayward's emergency line. I report what I have just witnessed, giving the street name and town. I feel like I have finally accomplished something useful for a change. We choose a quiet restaurant where we can drink wine and converse without a barrage of voices in the background. Thank you, Gloria.

Tuesday, April 4th

What will Sam's latest update be today when I let myself in through the back door of Dad's home? My commute is always an emotional challenge. I'll just drive around the block one more time to boost my courage and delay my entrance.

As I open the door, Sam quickly informs me, "Mr. C's penis is bleeding and full of pus. I've cleaned it as best as I could and bandaged it." Oh well, I find myself thinking, he doesn't need it anymore anyway. He hasn't been able to urinate for months, let alone make love. She continues her morning update. "His colostomy bag was full of runny green gunk when I changed it this morning," Sam prattles on. "And—he seems to have trouble swallowing anything but liquid today, says his throat is too tight. He immediately throws up anything he takes by mouth accompanied with the same substance that is accumulating in his colostomy bag." *I should have driven around the block six more times; I am not ready for this.* I also wonder why I have to be told all the gory details.

Sam manages to settle Dad in his recliner. He tries to make a telephone call using the TV remote. Both of us look at him, aghast. This is awful to watch. He must be having strokes? I bring the portable phone and put it into his hand. He can't find the right buttons to make his call. I help him locate the numbers, but he is confused and can't figure out how to stop the beep, beep, beep, screaming at him.

Dad sits very quietly, not lashing out at anyone. I can see by the deep grimace on his face, he knows something else is wrong with him, but can't figure it out. He can't form the right words to ask questions, but he keeps trying. Sam and I lovingly and gently try to finish his sentences and anticipate his needs. Even though he's not making any sense, we agree with everything he tries to say. We certainly don't want to aggravate him any further.

Lunchtime arrives and Sam brings Dad some yogurt. He picks up the spoon but can't locate his mouth. After a couple of misses, I carefully take the carton and spoon from him and begin to feed him. There is no argument. Only a look of relief and a quiet, "Thank you."

My son David returned this morning after completing his business and art deadlines in Florida and Jamaica. He is greatly distressed at seeing the decline in his grandfather during his short absence. Sadly David remarks to me, "I can't even make Papa smile or laugh anymore. We had such a wonderful time only a couple of months ago."

David and I use the excuse of another warm day to retreat

to the back yard. It feels wonderful to be out of the house. After five nurseries I finally located several bags of chicken manure, vegetables, and some flowers to plant around his mailbox. It seems Dad's comment the other day, that we were behind schedule, had some validity. Most people have already planted their gardens. David does the heavy labor, working the nutrients into the clay soil. It feels good to physically use my body and to feel the warm sun on my back. If I am needed inside—all Sam has to do is yell out the door.

While I am planting the tomatoes, a florist van pulls up in front of the house. "How thoughtful, someone is sending Dad a pretty arrangement of spring flowers," I tell David. Sam asks me to come inside. The note accompanying the beautiful bouquet is addressed to me. The flowers are from Joe. What a wonderful surprise. They are so fragrant, almost completely masking the smells of illness that have filled this house. It is just what I need to remind me yet again I am not alone. Even though we are living miles apart, Joe and I are handling this together.

Later in the afternoon, David orders a pizza while I settle myself at Dad's desk and pay a couple of his bills. After the pizza, I gather up my belongings and look for the envelopes I recently addressed to take to the post office…but I haven't a clue where I put them. My rummaging around the house and shuffling papers is irritating Dad. I sure can't let him know I've misplaced his bills. I can't imagine what has become of them. Frustrated and exhausted, I leave the searching for tomorrow and head back 'home' to my brother's.

Wednesday, April 5th

"Mr. C woke up vomiting this morning," Sam relates to me from Dad's bedroom as she holds a cool washcloth to his forehead. "I mashed up his pills so he could swallow them." Slowly Sam manages to put Dad into his wheelchair and prop him in his recliner. The oxygen has followed him. His color is better than yesterday, so looks like he might be more lucid. But when he tries to enter into conversations, his words and ideas don't fit.

The hospice nurse had come and gone an hour before I arrived. She'd admonished Sam for not calling hospice yesterday, Sam tells me. "Whenever you see a drastic change in Clarence," she scolded, "hospice should always be notified, no matter what time of the day." Sam and I agree with her decision, we didn't feel anyone would have been able to help with Dad's confusion yesterday.

I give Sam a deserved afternoon off. David continues working in the vegetable garden. I sit next to Dad's recliner in Mother's rocker. I'm afraid to leave the room. Afraid to leave Dad alone. He is still confused between the remote control and the telephone, but there is no outward display of anger. Perhaps he just doesn't have the energy. I have a new novel in my lap; hoping it will take my mind off this ugly scene.

Bill comes for his afternoon visit. "Bill, I missed the visiting nurse this morning, but I want to talk with her directly, not hear it from Sam."

"I fully agree, let's call hospice while Sam is away." We need an expert opinion on what is going on and what we can do to help, not just Sam's word. We put in the call to hospice and ask for a one-on-one conference. They quickly agree to come out and talk with us. Wow, Sam must have really upset the apple cart this morning to have someone come out when there's no emergency.

Our favorite nurse arrives just as Sam is pulling into the driveway. Oh, dear. I can see Sam is surprised and perhaps hurt by our actions. We were hoping to have this meeting before she returned.

I tell the nurse Dad's strokes have made it difficult for him to swallow. Almost everything, including medications, comes right back up. She agrees we need a stronger medication to keep Dad comfortable. She wants us to eliminate all medications except for pain and to begin morphine patches. They will be waiting for me at the pharmacy first thing in the morning.

Quietly, and away from my father, the nurse goes over the signs to look for in the last stages of life. We have read the hospice booklet, but it is comforting to have her talk to us about these symptoms. I can see Dad is experiencing many of them. He could die today or last another two weeks. It is amazing he has hung on for so long.

The nurse walks down the hallway to Dad's chair and talks to him about the changes going on in his body. As always, she is honest and up front with him, and answers all his questions.

"Mr. C is extending his life because he needs to accept Jesus Christ as his savior," Sam sits me down and declares after the nurse has left. "That's the reason God has called me to be with your father. You see, when Mr. C was born, and as a young person, he knew his path and he knew the truth. But he has gotten lost along the way with some new and different ideas in the Unitarian Church. He has lost the truth, which has made him afraid of death," She continues on in a dramatic voice. "God has called me to help him find the truth again! As soon as he accepts Jesus, he will be able to die peacefully."

After visiting his church last Sunday and having heard no mention of God or Jesus during the service, I guess she is convinced Dad is going straight to Hell and needs to realize this before it is too late.

I am seething with anger, but I sit here listening to her in silence. I don't dare discuss this with Sam. There is no way I want to antagonize Dad's caregiver. Dad believes strongly in a higher power. Dad and I have had so many wonderful discussions about God the last couple of years. He may not call this higher being 'God' all the time, for he is convinced the God so often spoken of and feared in most churches is NOT God. He believes in a much larger Deity than the one so often preached about on Sundays. Dad and I agree; there is no right path, but many paths leading to God.

My husband, feeling I need a break and quiet space for a couple of nights, has made reservations for me at a lovely hotel on the

Berkeley Marina. But I cancel them. I just can't get my act together to even pack a suitcase. It is easier to continue living on the floor in the same corner of Bill's living room.

Thursday April 6th

Dad's sentences are still only two or three words today. He can't follow conversations very well, but he is managing to be understood. He spends most of the day sleeping. When he picks up a book to read he promptly closes his eyes. He turns on the TV, and falls asleep. Sam says his kidneys are shutting down. He says he is not in pain. At this point we count that as a real blessing.

I dig in the vegetable garden while awaiting the nurse's now daily visit. It feels so good with the nourished soil David has created. I let it flow through my fingers, stay here for hours. I want to finish planting the vegetables, but I am having difficulty remembering which "X" in Dad's drawing means tomatoes and which represents the beans. Nevertheless, I say a blessing for each plant as I carefully submerge the roots in the fresh soil. Sam works all morning washing and ironing my clothes. What a nice gift. I don't know where she finds the energy.

Dad's nurse arrives in the early afternoon. No matter how he is feeling, he still enjoys joking and flirting with this lady, pretending he isn't as bad off as he appears.

As our nurse drives away I feel myself falling apart. I don't seem to be the strong person I once thought I was. Tears loom behind every thought and word. It's becoming more difficult to keep them under control. Much as I have been living with this reality, the whole idea that my father will not be here much longer has suddenly hit me. I won't receive any more phone calls on Sunday night as he runs through his week's events. I won't be dancing with him at the clubhouse socials, or sharing a bottle of Merlot on his deck. I thought I had prepared myself for this journey. Hot tears once again run down my cheeks; I will really miss that man.

I have tried to process life at arm's length. The last four months I have lived only for the moment, thinking little of the past and nothing about the future. I didn't want to get so fully immersed with Dad's illness and the process of his dying that I couldn't cope. I thought this would be like other situations I have had to handle in my life. One day I am asked to carry around an extra twenty pounds. Several days later I am told I need to carry forty pounds or I won't succeed. Of course I carry the extra weight even though it becomes a struggle. But the next day, much to my surprise, I am told in order to hang in there, I must carry sixty pounds more. Daily, the extra weight on my back becomes more difficult to bear until I can no longer support it. I am collapsing under the burden. I feel it crushing my lungs. I am having trouble just putting one foot in front of the other one. I am not even sure I will be able to get out of my bed tomorrow.

Friday, April 7th

This is the second day for the morphine patches. Dad is receiving a lower dose of the pain medication, but there have been no complaints. He appears to be more coherent and alert; able to form full sentences and carry on a conversation today. In fact, he looks and sounds better than he has for the last two weeks! This man must have nine lives. But then, how could I have expected less from my father? His roller-coaster is not running out of steam, but gathering momentum. It is racing faster and faster up and down the mountains and valleys of Dad's last days.

Our hospice nurse arrives first thing in the morning. She examines Dad. "Do not move Clarence into his wheelchair unless there is someone on either side. Sam, do not move him by yourself."

Sam is adamant. "I can help him into his chair by myself; I don't need anyone else."

"His legs are so infested with cancer," she tells us outside Dad's room, "I am afraid they will not be able to support him, and he could easily break his legs." I assure the nurse I will be around to help Sam.

Her visit over, the nurse and I meet outside for our private conference. It is easier to talk out here. I can get my questions answered and receive the reassurance I so desperately need. Beginning on Monday, she tells me, Dad will probably be confined to bed for the duration. But for the next couple of days however, we need to continue his routines. Once he is restricted to his bedroom, he will understand the fight is truly over.

"I can feel the cancer tumors all around your father's intestines and abdomen," the nurse continues. "This leaves him only a small opening for nourishment." She reiterates once again what we are to do when he begins to vomit uncontrollably. I realize she never says, "If," only "when" he begins to vomit.

"Use the pills I have given you and put one under his tongue. Have Sam give him suppositories and squirt a dropper full of liquid morphine in his cheek." But her litany of dread is not over. "There will be no IVs ordered even though he will be dehydrated. The IVs would only feed the tumors and not do anything to hydrate him. It won't be long now." We embrace. I am so grateful for her thorough explanations and her honesty, as well as her obvious concern about our well-being as caregivers.

I watch Dad read and doze in his chair. Bill is outside painting the shutters. I have contracted with a company to replace the deck, steps, and roof next week. We know we will have to sell this place shortly.

Mary comes for her visit. She pushes Dad's wheelchair to the deck to enjoy the warmth of the spring day. They hold hands. Few words are exchanged. The meaning in their silence expresses it all. She is becoming too uncomfortable with his declining health. She lingers for only an hour, looking grateful to be able to retrace her steps and return to the comfort of her own home. Dad resumes his position in his recliner after Sam and I both help him.

I feel like I am next to a time bomb. When will Dad begin vomiting? I'm not sure why I am not vomiting or why my stomach has survived with the abuse I've given it the last couple of months. My lunch is usually just bread and cheese and too many cookies, and TV dinners in the evening with a couple of glasses of wine. And, of course, more cookies or pieces of candy during the day. I keep feeding my overgrowing body. I'll just have to deal with this issue later. Dad can't eat anything, I am eating for the two of us, just stuffing it in, the food and my frayed emotions.

Bill comes in to sit with Dad while I go outside to plant a couple more vegetables. The garden is almost complete. I need poles and string for the beans and will have to remind myself to water each day. We give Sam the opportunity to take a few hours on her own since Bill and I plan to spend Saturday by ourselves. We are nervous and frightened at the thought of being here alone with Dad. But we smile anyway as we tell Sam goodbye. "Have a wonderful afternoon off. We'll be just fine." The two of us sit in the living room and keep Dad under close surveillance.

"Dad, Joe is coming out again to see you!" A warm smile spreads across Dad's face as I relay this information. I am not sure how my husband can maintain his job and still support me 3,000 miles away, but I am not complaining. When he comes, even for a short visit, it means we stay in a motel. Not a fancy one, but a real room with real beds and a TV I can turn on any time I choose. The two of us can even go out to dinner at a nice restaurant.

I end the day answering my emails on Dad's computer.

"Dear Leslie," I read,

"Our prayers still go up, and all we can know is that when God thinks everyone has done what they need to do, the end will be peaceful and acceptable. Grief will be brief, but wonderful memories will take over and the healing will begin. Memories are precious and uplifting."

Saturday April 8th

Bill and I 'sneak' out of his condo before eight o'clock. We feel like school children off to play hooky. I love collecting old postcards. Today there is a postcard show in Santa Cruz, a beach community, a two and a half hour drive away. What a great diversion—yippee!

The weather has held and there is very little traffic this morning. It is so nice letting Bill be responsible for the driving. We know each other so well that lapses in our conversation, or interjected, unrelated topics only deepen the bond between us.

Arriving before the start of the show, we buy take-out coffee and settle on a deserted bench along the boardwalk. We sip our drinks, watching and listening to the waves beat against the sandy shore under the morning fog. The smell of the salty sea and moist air is invigorating and refreshing. A few sea gulls call to us overhead, the only call we hope to have today. Sam knows we desperately need to get away. She has assured us she can handle anything that might come her way. I check my cell phone; confirm it is on. Bill also pulls out his pager, scrutinizes the read out. No, he has not missed a call.

We spend the morning happily browsing through rows of postcards, spending money ruthlessly. This is almost as good as a sugar high. I am sure somewhere up on a shelf behind the last box of cards in the last booth is the one card I have been searching for to complete the book I am writing using postcards as illustrations; the book I have had to put on hold.

We break for a quick lunch. We don't want to waste time eating when there are still stacks and stacks of unexplored cards out there. Over sandwiches and iced tea, we talk about the show, the dealers, the weather, and share the postcards we have purchased. We don't mention Dad. He isn't here today. However, I pull out my phone time and time again, just to make sure I haven't inadvertently turned it off.

During the long drive home, the holiday feeling we enjoyed earlier is replaced with dread. Fewer words are exchanged. We each have to silently prepare for what might be waiting for us. The closer to Hayward we get, the more apprehensive we become. Normal congestion has filled the highway. Bill's anger erupts explosively as cars weave in and out of our lane of traffic. His swear words fill the car like black, smelly smoke from someone's cheap cigar. We need to let this growing tension escape but we don't want to let in the ugliness of what might be looming ahead, so the windows remain rolled up and in place.

When we arrive, we find Sam in the kitchen fixing dinner, salmon she purchased yesterday. The aroma is inviting. She has gone to a lot of trouble to make everything special for us. But along with the mouthwatering smells of dinner are her words, "Mr. C has had a bad day. He had an upset stomach most of the day and is very distressed about the oozing from his incision and penis."

Bill and I walk to the recliner to speak with Dad. Sam takes care of the last preparations for dinner. Dad's mouth is turned down in that all too familiar angry grimace. He has the hiccups. He doesn't say anything; but Bill and I know he is yelling loudly internally, "How dare you two leave me all day? How dare you two go and have fun while I am here suffering and in pain? You promised me you would be here, Leslie. Where were you?"

During dinner Sam shares her day with us as Dad remains in his recliner. I take a fresh bite of salmon and hear, "He is now having a bloody discharge from his rectum accompanied by a very nasty odor. He keeps feeling like he needs to have a bowel movement." *At this point my dinner is spoiled.*

To camouflage Dad's growing anger we can feel seeping in from the living room, Sam continues to carry on a lengthy conversation. She tries laughing and giggling to lighten the surroundings. It doesn't work. Dad's sour expression doesn't change while sitting in his recliner. I can no longer handle his hostile feelings from across the room, nor the litany from Sam. I plead exhaustion from our long day.

We leave Sam alone to deal with the kitchen clutter and Dad's turmoil. Bill and I drive back to Oakland, relieved to just be heading away. When we arrive, Kathy greets me with a smile and a rented video, a chick-flick for the two of us. Just a fun, light-hearted movie aimed at women. We pop popcorn, rest our tired bodies and minds, gladly following the adventures of make-believe characters through light and funny episodes.

Sunday, April 9

With a mixture of dread and absolute need, I pull into Dad's driveway at noon; I am much later than usual. It has taken awhile to pull myself together today. After last evening's ordeal I have had to take time to convince myself it is my duty to go and see my father.

"Oh, he doesn't care whether I am there or not," I tell myself. "All he wants is someone to yell at."

"No, it is the illness. He really is not shouting directly at you, well he is, but he is really crying out at the cancer. You remember, Leslie, how in control he has always needed to be? He now must depend on all of us. How awful it must to be for someone with Dad's personality Don't be so hard on him or on yourself. One moment at a time. This won't last forever. Come on, Leslie, you can do it, one more day."

And on and on. The voice in my mind never takes a break. It urges me on to make this ugly drive just one more time.

Today is the organ concert, the one Dad was so concerned about last Sunday. As soon as I open the back door, he quickly informs me he wants to attend the concert. He loves organ music. Getting to see the people in the park as well as the organ club members will be a real boost for him, he tells me.

I settle myself in Mother's chair, pulling it close to him so I can hold his hand. Gently, looking into his crestfallen face, I explain, "Dad, people will understand that you can't make it this time." I am sure the exertion will make him terribly sick to his stomach, to say nothing of the awful night he will probably experience afterwards.

"You have orchestrated the entire event, and thanks to you, the guest musician is now familiar with Mom's organ. All the club members were called and the park residents have been notified."

After several more persuasive comments, he finally agrees with me. It is as though he needed me to tell him not to go, to put my foot down. He relaxes and settles back in his chair, looking relieved that he doesn't have to put forth energy he doesn't have.

"I know I don't have much time left, Leslie. I am at the end."

"I know, Dad."

"I want to make sure; Bill, my grandchildren, and Joe, do they all know my condition?"

"Yes, Dad. They all know. So you can let go anytime. You have been holding on to this small thread of life that grows thinner and more fragile every day for too long now. You need to let it go, Dad."

"Yes, I know that. I have been holding on to every bit of life I could possibly grab. I don't need to do that any longer. I don't want to do that any longer. I just want to go now."

"Go for the light, Dad. Close your eyes and let yourself go toward the bright, luminous glow. When you cross over, there will be a warm barbecued steak simmering on a plate waiting for you and a fine bottle of aged Merlot. It will be so wonderful you will wonder why the heck you waited so long. You're not leaving us, just your worn-out, diseased body; you'll always be with us no matter where you are. And we will always be with you; we will always love you."

He closes his eyes and I see the muscles in his face relax. I continue to hold his hand. My hand begins to cramp in the awkward position, but I don't want to let go of the love and warmth we have just shared.

I offer to go to the concert in his place. I promise to update him, report on the caliber of the music, the organist, and who was in the audience. *How difficult to go to the clubhouse alone right now.*

I call Mary so I will have company. We sit together on the folding chairs and converse softly. The new president of the organ club climbs the two steps to the stage. Using the microphone, she announces, "Clarence Compton will not be presiding today. I have taken over for him. He is not doing well with his battle with cancer."

I can't believe the organist Dad met with last week, who practiced all Sunday afternoon, couldn't make the concert. I also can't believe his replacement is the man I hired to play for Mom and Dad's 60th anniversary party. This organist will be very familiar with Mom's organ, he gave her lessons for a few years.

The first musical number fills the hall as I fight back hot tears. I concentrate on listening to the familiar sounds of Mother's organ and enjoy the show of pleasure in those around me. Putting the music in the background, my eyes slowly rove the auditorium.

> We celebrated Mom and Dad's 60th anniversary right in this very room. Garlands of paper hung from the rafters. Paper hearts and flowers decorated the windows. We set up the folding tables and decorated them in pink ribbon and violets. Mother loved violets. The head table was positioned in front of the stage. A small table was placed to the left with an on-going video Bill carefully orchestrated, pictures of Mom and Dad's sixty years together. Next to the TV, were newspaper copies of wedding pictures and their announcement. To the right of the stage was another table with their first three-tiered wedding cake. My parents eloped sixty years ago; they didn't have a wedding cake. When the time came to cut the cake, Mother took great pleasure in shoving a huge piece into Dad's mouth. You can see the pleasure in her face captured in the picture Kathy snapped. The organist I hired brought his own portable keyboards. He played and sang songs from the thirties and forties. There was laughter that day, memories renewed, hugs from endearing friends and family members who traveled far for the celebration. The caterer did a fine job, the food was delicious.

Mother looked so pretty in the new turquoise silk blouse I bought for her. I'd manicured her nails and painted them with a pretty pink polish. Digging through her jewelry drawer, I found the three-string pearl necklace Dad gave her when he was in the service that she'd never worn. She was always saving it for 'that special occasion.' Well, this was a special occasion, and I insisted she put it on. Dad dressed in his best dress shirt, sport coat, and a clip-on tie. Afterwards we had family over to the house to continue the celebration with some libation.

I am suddenly aware the music has ended. The concert is over. Clapping and cheering are all around me. Slowly remembering where I am, I join the throng of applause. People are leaving their chairs and I am quickly bombarded with questions.

"How is your father doing?"
"Oh, that's too bad."
"How much longer?"
"Is he on morphine yet?"
"Is he with hospice?"
"Is he still at home?"
"Who is with him right now?"

Questions are thrown at me from people who do not feel comfortable calling or coming for a visit. Before long I thank them for their concern and head back to report to Dad.

While critiquing the concert I can see a pronounced physical change in my father. With his eyes closed, he looks like he has finally given up, turned loose his hold on life. He is ready to go on. He opens his eyes, finally aware of my presence.

"I've been having the strangest dreams while you were at the concert. When I doze I encounter many of my grammar school and high school classmates who are long gone. Why, I haven't even thought about them for years. Do you suppose that means it's almost my time?"

"Yes, Dad. I think you are really communicating with your friends and they are waiting for you, to welcome you to a place where there is no pain."

He drops off to sleep again, with a peaceful, resigned look on his face. I push back Mom's chair, gather my purse, and head back to Bill's. Before I leave, Sam has to lift Dad into his wheelchair to move him into the kitchen area. We exchange quick eye contact. Dad can no longer stand on his legs. It looks like the nurse was right after all. He will probably be confined to his bed from here on out.

Once again exhausted, I collapse into bed early. Bill and I sleep restlessly in separate sections of his house, convinced tonight Dad will cash it all in.

Monday, April 10th

There was no phone call last night. Bill and I want this to be over. We both want the phone to ring, telling us the end has finally come. And yet, we are still not ready to deal with the loss.

Dad is not in his recliner this morning, nor is he in his wheelchair eating applesauce at the counter. He is still in bed. The hospice nurse is examining him when I arrive. I listen discreetly to the conversation from the hallway.

"Clarence, you will have to stay in bed from now on. I'm sorry. Your legs are too weak and too infested with cancer to hold you any longer. I am worried about bone breakage. You would really complicate matters if you broke a leg." I listen but hear no response from Dad. I'm sure he expected this news. But it doesn't make it easier to accept.

Bed. Never to sit in his favorite chair to watch people walk by his house or to keep track of activities going on around him. One more piece of Dad's life has been taken. Not much more can be eliminated except life itself. Soon nothing will be left but memory.

The end is near. His silence tells me he is quietly processing this new information. He is angry, but giving himself a talking to, "That's life, that's just the way life is."

The nurse hugs me on her way out of Dad's bedroom. She then calls the doctor, who agrees to increase the morphine patches to two a day. When I go in to see Dad, he tells me he wants his bed to be moved to the family room. He needs to feel he is still part of the family. I call the health agency. "Sorry, we can't come out there and dismantle his bed, move it, and set it up again. His insurance won't cover that cost. It has to stay where it is." *Damn it!*

"Dad, I'm sorry but the health agency will not come and move your bed. But I think I know a way to make you feel better about being back here. Just hang in there."

I am going to transform his bedroom. I bring in his get-well cards and letters from the living room and scotch tape them all over the walls. There are so many, it looks like new wallpaper. I cut the few roses that have cautiously decided to bloom in his back yard, arrange them in vases, and place them where he can see them without turning his head. I push a table close to his bed. I bring in a light, his bottle of water, a phone, a pencil, and a pad of paper from the living room. Next, I carry the TV and place it on his chest of drawers and give him the remote. I make a mental note to buy some brightly colored balloons tomorrow to fill an empty corner. I move the indoor plants from the living room into his bedroom. I want his visitors to feel as comfortable as possible and I don't want Dad to feel isolated. A few hours later and the room looks altogether different.

He smiles at me. "Thank you," he softly says. He likes what I have done to brighten up his space. A good feeling for both of us.

Believe it or not, Dad seems more alert today. He hasn't had to use any precious energy this morning to dress, brush teeth, shave, move into his wheelchair, and then move into his recliner. With a sheepish grin he informs me, "I plan to stick around for two more weeks." I'm not sure why he has decided on a two-week plan. His whole body is in pain. But he doesn't want to take too much morphine. He wants to be alert and able to converse with his visitors, especially Mary.

With a small dose of morphine in his cheek, Dad proceeds to tell me what to do next in his vegetable garden. "Okay," I tell him. "The weather is good; I understand the program." David and I go outside and work a while in the garden, a garden where no one will experience its rewards. For no matter how beautifully it blooms, we know it will be a fruitless effort. But it must help Dad to have something around him growing and flourishing. After two hours of digging and planting, I come inside for a break. Before I can sit down, Dad informs me that it is time to clean out his desk, which is in the spare bedroom where Sam sleeps.

"I want you to pull out one drawer at a time. Bring it into the bedroom so we can go through the contents together. I need to make sure you know where things go and what can and can't be thrown out after I am gone." I already know these details; yet I'm sure this makes him feel better. He is taking care of things. He's still in charge.

An organ club member comes to see Dad. "Clarence, I was able to tape yesterday's organ concert for you." *I wasn't aware anyone was taping the music. How very thoughtful!* Dad's only good tape deck is attached to his stereo system in the living room. "Sam, can you set up your portable boom-box so we can hear the organ concert?" No sooner do we voice this request than she appears with the tape player. Hearing the familiar organ that was mother's and memorable music of the 40's seems to soothe Dad and helps him to rest. Very little sleep last night and the concert yesterday have worn me out. I realize how very, very tired I am.

Dad's minister visits after lunch. The plans for his memorial service are almost complete. We don't mention the epitaph Dad was hoping to finish. Perhaps he has forgotten. David, Sam, and I join hands around Dad's bed and the minister leads us in prayer. I wish there was more mention of God in the minister's prayers, but she does seem to calm Dad, and that's what is important.

He drifts off to sleep and his mouth drops open. I watch him for a couple of minutes. He has never slept that way before. His mouth is wide open, and his jaw has dropped as though it has become unhinged. If I didn't see a slight breathing movement through his sheet, I would think he had passed on. *So that is what he will look like dead.*

Late in the afternoon I tell Dad goodbye. "I love you, Dad. I'll be back in the morning." It comforts me to know that if he dies tonight, the last thing I have said to him is, "I love you."

Before leaving, I retrieve my emails from Dad's computer and look forward to hearing from my husband.

"I finally found the photo we need for the memorial service, of Pappy at the beach with his camera!! It was in a box of other photos of your mom and dad that had been put in a drawer of the server cabinet in our kitchen area. There are no coincidences. I had just given up and was getting ready to go to bed. I had lit a candle to hold your dad in my consciousness earlier in the day, and decided to look for the brass candlesnuffer to put it out. Holding him very much in my mind, I began a search for the snuffer. Looked first in the china cabinet, then in the server. The drawer to the right had candle stuff, but no snuffer, so I opened the left drawer and there was a brown envelope with the picture we needed of Pappy lying on top!"

Tuesday, April 11th

Dad is still with us. Why am I surprised? He said he had two more weeks on this earth! He spends the day resting, using his oxygen continuously.

David and I spend most of the morning weeding around the new vegetables. The rest of the morning, I busy myself cleaning up the living room now that Dad will no longer need it.

THAT'S JUST THE WAY LIFE IS...

In the afternoon I take his car for its 12,000-mile service. I know I will be there a while, so I bring a book and look forward to some quiet time without guilt feelings. When I arrive, the TV is on overhead and servicemen are coming in and out of the waiting area. Different people enter, others leave to retrieve their cars and the rest of us wait. I find it relaxing sitting in the middle of this group, waiting for their cars to be serviced. Everyone enters wearing brightly colored clothes and no one carries a stethoscope! What a delightful place. I'll have to come here more often.

I return to Dad's and say goodbye for the day. He is sitting up eating his supper of beef broth flavored mashed potato and applesauce. Sam tells me he eats very little now, but still enjoys some yogurt during the day and an occasional cup of hot tea.

I am struggling with Sam living here and taking care of my father. She is doing an outstanding job. No one could do better. But many things disturb me and I know it must have to do with another woman living in Dad's house. If Mary had moved in, I think I might still feel the same way. I want Sam to operate Mom's washer and dryer as Mom did. The way she taught me. You know, *the right way*. And don't put her precious cookware in the dishwasher! Mother always scrubbed those with Brillo pads, to make them shine and glisten. Not in the dishwasher, they will turn ugly.

I tread lightly around Sam. I couldn't do the 24-hour job she is doing, even if I was medically qualified. But every time I try to assist Dad in some physical way, she intervenes. She feels it is her job to care for him without any help from me.

"I'll take care of that, Leslie."

"No, Sam, I want to do it myself!"

"No, Leslie. I will take care of this."

"Damn it! No, Sam. He is my father!" I want to say. I pull back rather than make a scene. Dad certainly doesn't need two women squabbling over his care.

Sam talks to me constantly. She tries to lighten up the prevailing gloom hanging over this house by sharing little tidbits of her life. I work hard to bite my tongue, appearing like a snob and probably not too friendly. She offers to cook for me each night and I usually turn her down. I know it must be difficult for her to eat alone, but I need to escape. I want my wine and my little space on the floor in Bill's living room.

I talk with our hospice nurse about my confusion and mixed feelings.

"I don't want to feel this way toward Sam," I tell her. "How can I see things differently and control my feelings?" The nurse gives me a blank stare.

"Leslie, you are such a special person, so strong, and so in control."

She is puzzled that I would even have this kind of a complaint. The other day I mentioned my concerns to Dad's minister and received the same reaction. I won't discuss this with them again, I decide. I will just keep these feelings bottled up inside and deal with them at a later time.

But as a last resort I decide to talk about my feelings with my brother and sister-in-law. Kathy has the same reaction as the other two women.

"Well, Leslie, if Sam's washing your clothes bothers you, just do them at our house, what's the big deal?" And, "It is always difficult to have two women in one kitchen. You don't have to drink her coffee or eat her muffins or watch her clean the dishes."

In exasperation I loudly explode, "It isn't the coffee, the muffins, the wash, or the food. It is what surrounds all of those. If I took those helping, considerate things away, there would still be something weird there!"

All of a sudden Bill understands. "It's like the *Body Snatchers*," he exclaims. "She's climbing into our lives to become one of us. Sam is suddenly taking over because she doesn't have a life or home of her own." *Invasion of the Body Snatchers.* Suddenly this all falls into place and I feel a great sense of relief.

* * *

I am drifting farther and farther away; away from the person I thought I was, to a no-man's island. I feel like I no longer do anything that is uniquely me. I wear the same clothes, perform the same activities, and drive in Dad's car, following the same route, day after day. I am afraid when this is all over I won't be able to resume my life. I have forgotten what my existence was all about. Was I traveling on a worthwhile pilgrimage? Or was my life just an illusion; routines to keep me busy to feel productive? I don't think I have the energy to care anymore or to figure it out—I am totally spent. What is going to happen to me? The only protection I know is to retreat into myself to preserve what little is left of the person I used to know. I must remain emotionless. I'll climb out again a few years from now and see if the sun is shining.

Wednesday, April 12th

Heavy black rain clouds blew in last night. It is a gray, depressing morning. I stop by a florist and pick up a bouquet of brightly colored Mylar balloons. Before getting out of the car at Dad's place, I work to untangle the strings of the balloons while holding on to them so none will escape when I open the car door. Hearing me arrive, Sam opens the back door to inform me. "This is not a good day for Mr. C." *Oh God, here we go again!* "He is complaining of pain everywhere and has been given some break-through morphine." This means Dad will sleep most of the day.

I arrange the bright colors of Mylar in a corner that Dad can easily view from his bed. He weakly smiles his approval. I take my mystery novel and Mom's chair into his room and settle next to his bed. Because of the change in the weather, his windows are closed.

No more fresh air. I sit and try to read, but my eyes rove over the same paragraph, time after time. There is a terrible smell permeating Dad's bedroom. It reminds me of ammonia or a strong bathroom mold remover. The odor burns my eyes and irritates my nose. I can only sit for 45 minutes before I have to step outside.

"What is that smell, Sam?"

"It is the cancer and the smell of death seeping through his pores."

I have never smelled cancer before. I have only heard about the vile odor. Does Dad smell it? How awful to realize you reek with such a rotten smell. Sam also tells me his urine bag is now filled with a cheesy substance. Another sign the end is very near.

Joe is flying into San Francisco tonight to spend a couple of days with us. Dad is so looking forward to this visit. I know he'll hang on until he has seen his beloved son-in-law one more time.

In the afternoon, Mary comes for her routine visit. Dad rallies from his stupor and the ugly smell vanishes without a trace, interesting what the human mind can do. What an amazing mechanism, our bodies.

I leave early in the evening to let Dad drift in and out of a deep sleep. Once at Bill's, I pack a suitcase for the next couple of days, clean up a little, and leave to meet my husband at the airport.

As I pull out of Bill's driveway, the dismal gray clouds, now full of moisture, open up and drench the Bay Area. Maneuvering a car across the San Mateo Bridge in blackness is bad enough, but with torrential rains, visibility is a joke. I will make it to the airport with no mishaps, I tell myself. Dad wants to see Joe again. I just have to make all of this happen. I concentrate on relaxing my hands around the steering wheel and let Spirit guide me.

I arrive to find Joe's flight time has once again been delayed an hour because of the weather. I sit at the familiar well-lit circular bar, right in front of the arrival gate. I people watch, and order some cold chardonnay. The cold, wet wine glass feels delightful to hold.

I have safely arrived and don't have to think or do anything for the next hour. I stare blankly at strangers talking non-stop on their cell phones, some running frantically to catch planes, others warmly hugging loved ones carrying backpacks, briefcases, or overnight bags. Joe is coming. All will be well. I won't have to worry any longer. He will be the one to navigate the way to our reserved motel room.

Thursday, April 13th

After an early breakfast, Joe and I drive the short distance to Dad's. I am amazingly aware that yesterday's ugly cancer smell is no longer present. Dad is sitting up in bed. He is alert, shaved, and has brushed his teeth and hair—in anticipation of seeing Joe. During their visit, he continues to ask for break-through morphine. Dad does not want to be in pain and waste this precious time with my husband.

We sit with Dad as he has a breakfast of cream of wheat, a small piece of cantaloupe, and some hot tea. Joe sits with him through lunchtime and helps him eat a smoothie David concocts from banana, cantaloupe, and yogurt. From the living room, I hear snatches of conversation as the two men replay memories of times spent together. Between intermittent visits to the vegetable garden to work on the watering system and fixing small problems around the house, Joe again sits with Dad while he eats his dinner of broth and mashed potatoes.

Dad is visibly tired. Joe, David, and I prepare to leave, hoping to find a quiet restaurant to be together—alone. "Get some rest, Dad. We'll come see you before we head back to our motel tonight."

The Bay Area is a busy place no matter what day of the week. Almost every restaurant has a 30-minute wait. We just want a simple meal, nothing fancy. An hour and a half later, driving around trying to find a decent place, the level of our voices grow louder with frustration.

"Who cares where we eat? I'm just hungry. McDonalds?"

"There has to be something better than that around here," pipes Joe.

"Well, if we don't find something soon, we'll have to look for a gas station. This is ridiculous!"

We finally settle on a no-name café. There is no wait at this restaurant. The reason becomes very clear as the plates of greasy food are set down before us.

During dinner, Joe tells me he has made an offer on a house outside of Boston. The offer will probably be accepted. He pulls out a picture from his briefcase to show me.

"Joe, this place looks huge, much too big for just the two of us. Didn't we drive by this house just last year?"

"The only downside to this place that I can see is that this house," he continues, "has no air conditioner and no fireplace."

This sounds crazy to me, living on the east coast. Something will have to be done before I move in. He promises to send me pictures of the interior so I can get a sense of where I will be going when this is all over. He thinks we may get to live there for two years. *Wow, two years, yippee!* I should be excited; we'll soon have our own home again. But right now, all I can feel is anger. This is just one more thing I have to deal with. I will never get to see the place before it is purchased. We rented a home when we moved a year ago from New York. I knew we needed to locate a place of our own, but couldn't this have waited? I feel totally discombobulated.

Dinner away from the house gives Joe and me the opportunity to thank our son David for all the support he has given his grandfather and me during this time. We also let him know that he needn't stay any longer. It's okay for him to go any time. He is so young to have to deal with this and he is visibly exhausted. "Papa is so grateful you have stayed so long. But he also wants you to go out and live your life, David," I tell him. "Go, when you feel you need to."

It is close to ten o'clock by the time we finish our 'delightful' meal.

"No sense in going in to see Dad tonight, it's too late," I announce to Joe and David. "We'll disturb his sleep. Besides, I am tired and just want to go to bed. He'll understand." We quietly ease into Dad's driveway, leave David on the back porch, and drive to our motel.

Ah, our motel! It will feel so good to get inside. We'll just relax, turn on the boob tube, and watch crazy re-runs. We unlock the door to our room and hear the phone blaring on the bedside table. I hate telephones! I run toward the sound as Joe turns on the lights.

"I've had a rough night," Dad says in a soft, shaky, frightened voice. "I thought you were stopping over after dinner. Please come over right away."

Oh, God, there goes our quiet night together. We extinguish the lights we so quickly turned on and rush out the door. I am frantic as we ride the short distance. We can't drive fast enough to suit me. What has happened to create this fear in his voice?

"No problem." Sam opens the back door for us. "Mr. C is just having a panic attack, happens to all my hospice patients. They suddenly realize that they are dying and it is final. No need to be concerned. I have been cradling and holding him most of the night."

But I am concerned and I am not happy. Sam didn't call me. Dad had to ask for the phone and the number of the motel himself. I should have been there for him. How selfish of me to go out to dinner while he was so uncomfortable! I should have been the one to hold and cradle my father, not some strange 'body snatcher'!

"You must stay by my bedside!" His temper is sizzling. "You did not stop to see me after dinner like you said you would." This anger continues to build, running over the brim of his already full cup. He is wired and acting like his morphine was mixed with a hallucinating upper. His eyes hold a wide-open stare.

"I am afraid if I close my eyes, I'll die." Once again, I feel I have failed my father.

"I promise, Dad, I will stay right here next to you until I know you are asleep, no matter how long it takes."

Sam continues to hold and rock him. In the bedside table is her portable tape deck. Hymns softly sung by a church choir fill Dad's bedroom. *Is this the kind of music Dad wants to hear?* Sitting on the other side of the bed, I gently take hold of his hand. Sam hums along with the music. By twelve-thirty AM, Dad finally falls into a deep sleep. I stay another half an hour to be sure he will not awaken. We turn out his lights and quietly leave the room. I am livid. I am tired. I am angry. I let Sam have a piece of my mind.

"Why didn't you call me? You must call me the minute there is any change. I don't give a damn if you feel you can handle the situation yourself or not. This is *my* father and I want to be here for him!"

On the way back to the motel Joe gives me a lecture about the politically correct way of handling this type of situation. He goes over the many ways I should have talked to Sam. "Go to Hell!" I yell back at him.

Friday, April 14th

Thank God the phone doesn't ring again after we finally collapse into bed. My frustration and anger cools after a few hours of deep sleep and a refreshing shower.

After a relaxing breakfast in our room we drive back to see Dad. The hospice nurse has already arrived. She increased his patches because of the constant pain. She is hoping to eliminate some of the breakthrough morphine. Dad sleeps. It is very apparent last night took its toll.

Poor Daddy, why does he have to suffer so? He has had to be so strong these last few years. He has had to call on incredible strength and power he didn't know he possessed.

> Five years ago began the downhill decline. Because of poor financial management, Mom and Dad were forced to move from their home of forty years in Orinda to a retirement

area to have easy access to shopping and doctors. Early that summer I flew to California to assist them with this life change.

The images will always be with me. Dad tirelessly going through slide carousels, boxes, and drawers full of camera equipment, and old photos. His photography days were over. Everything had to be sold and/or tossed that would not fit into their recently purchased used mobile home.

My brother and I helped our parents sort through their accumulated stash, organized a garage sale, a Goodwill drop, a trash pickup, find a realtor, and put the family home on the market. When all was accomplished, I flew back to New York to unpack the mounds of boxes stacked up in a house we had just purchased after moving from North Carolina. Unfortunately for me, their home sold more quickly than we had anticipated. One month later, I boarded a plane heading to the West Coast again to help my parents pack their belongings and move them into their adult mobile home park.

True to form, once they had moved, Dad worked diligently to make his mobile home comfortable. Out came the remaining tools to build bookcases. He strung cable wires under the house, installed a new heater, painted the whole inside, and put blinds on all the windows. He wasn't going to let the 'little things' of life get him down—ever. After all, "That's just the way life is." He was a fighter and a survivor. Nothing had taken him down before; he had always been tough enough to see life through.

In October of that same year I visited California again, this time to help them plan their 60th wedding anniversary celebration. But Mom wasn't doing very well. She had lost a lot of weight and was experiencing a continuous bladder infection no cocktail of antibiotics seem to touch. The following February she was diagnosed with bladder cancer. Dad took wonderful, loving, and tireless care of her at their home. She survived only until early May.

"How are you dealing with Mom's passing, Dad? You know hospice has wonderful programs for grieving spouses," I asked him a couple of months later during one of our weekly phone calls.

"I went to a couple of meetings, but I just wasn't feeling very sad, not like the others in the group. In fact I haven't spent much time grieving at all. I feel a little guilty about this. My feelings are more like relief, not grief."

"That's perfectly okay, Dad. You have to go with your feelings, pretending you feel something else doesn't do anyone any good."

His first purchases after he recovered from exhaustion as Mom's caregiver were a hearing aid, a new Saturn with a moon roof, and cataract surgery. I remember hearing about his joyous amazement at how brilliant the colors of flowers appeared, especially the blues, after his surgery. He traveled whenever his budget would allow. He joined and became active in the Unitarian church. He became a member of the Elks, tending bar during their Monday night football games and a 'hash slinger' during Saturday morning breakfasts. He was elected president of his Home Organ club, photographer for his mobile home park, and became a member of the security patrol helping to keep the area safe for its senior residents. The only problem he seemed to experience was loneliness during the evenings. This was soon eliminated when he met Mary, the sweet, petite, energetic widow down the street—no more lonely evenings for either one of them.

But this time it is different; he can't fight back. This time he will have to let go of everything . . . and move on.

* * *

Joe and I decide to leave Dad's place at noon. He is not really conscious that we are around. When awake, he is disoriented, not sure where he is. Unable to cope with the confusion, he closes his eyes and dozes in the middle of sentences. We are not doing anyone any good by sitting here all day watching him sleep, wondering when he will take his last breath. Joe and I decide to spend the rest of the day just being together. My husband assures Sam that he will have his cell phone turned on. We let her know, once again, she needs to call if there is a change or if Dad is asking for me. We're not going through a repeat performance of last night.

There are just a few scattered clouds floating around. It's a cool spring day complete with sweet clean smells that come after a good rain. We use Dad's car to meander through the back roads of Contra Costa County, revisiting homes where we once lived. It is a day trip through memory lane. We recall how we had viewed the future through rose-colored glasses of promise and opportunities. It is disconcerting to discover many of our favorite haunts have been replaced by new, ugly architecture with modern sharp lines. Today presents constant reminders that we can't go back, can't go home again.

Early evening finds us in Walnut Creek. We elect to eat dinner at an upscale seafood restaurant for a special treat. Seated at a table by a window per our request, I order wine and tell the waiter not to hurry with our order. We need some more time. *Please God, stop the clock and let me catch my breath.*

The quiet respite is wonderful. Because of the early hour, very few diners have arrived. We listen to an indoor waterfall in the background, gaze at the fading sunlight and pedestrians along the avenue. For just this brief moment it feels like God indeed has answered my prayers. Time has stopped. We have some precious moments together. It is wonderful to be with someone I know so well. We don't need a titillating conversation; silence is understood.

Our respite is over much too quickly. As soon as we head back, the wine's warm glow and the flavor of the mouth-watering salmon quickly vanish. I can feel my anxiety rising with every turn and twist in the road. Even though Joe's phone has not rung during our time together, I know it probably won't be a pleasant situation back at Dad's.

Preparing for the worst, Joe and I go into Dad's bedroom, each thankful for the other's support. We sit with my father until Sam is ready to prepare him for the night. We want to say goodbye and be on our way.

We move to the living room to await the signal from Sam that Dad has finally drifted off. Instead, he's having trouble getting to sleep again tonight. "Hurry, hurry in here!" he yells. Dad is experiencing another panic attack. I scoot the chair close to his bed, take his hand, tell him about our day, and recall memories all three of us have shared. It is eleven o'clock before Dad drops off to sleep. Once again, I emphasize to Sam how important it is for her to call us no matter what the hour, or if there is any change in his condition or he asks for me. We quietly slip out the back door.

Sunday April 16th

After breakfast we check out of our motel and drive to Dad's. Joe needs to say his goodbyes, he's flying home today.

Sam greets us on the back stoop with her report. "Mr. C's penis is now leaking urine." But Dad's had an ureterostomy. How could that even be possible? But I guess with cancer, everything horrific is possible.

Dad's fingers are so swollen he has difficulty grasping my husband's hand. Joe thanks Dad once again for being such a wonderful father. "And for all the wonderful memories that will live long after you are gone, Pappy." Listening to my husband put closure on a lifetime relationship, I weep quietly outside the doorway. Joe's short visit is over. We both know he will not see my father again.

Driving to San Francisco airport, I feel so thankful to have had a short time with my husband. I will constantly relive it in my mind, squeezing the last drop of healing juices from its memory.

After dropping off Joe at the airport, I go back to check on Dad. The morphine is finally doing its job and he's resting peacefully. I feel fairly comfortable driving to Bill's, no more panic attacks. I unpack my suitcase from the weekend, reorganize my area of the living room, and pour a glass of chilled wine. Every time the phone rings we all jump, dashing as quickly as possible to answer it . . . our nerves jangling, on fire.

Just as we are turning out our lights and heading for bed, the all too familiar ring jars us one more time. This late at night it sounds like a grating shriek, unlike the earlier high-pitched tone. It can only be an emergency. Kathy wins the race to the phone. Bill and I tensely gather around trying to hear the other side of the conversation.

"Mr. C was throwing up green vomit and shaking uncontrollably this evening."

"Should we come out?" Kathy glances at us.

"No," we hear Sam reply. "I called hospice. They have been out to see him and gave him more morphine. He is finally settling down now."

Kathy stands in the center of the room holding the receiver in her hand. The room is silent. We have nothing to say to one another. *Okay, where is our morphine to settle us down?* As tired as we are, we also know this will be a night of fitful sleep.

Monday April 17th

I struggle to maintain my sanity, filling my mind with sewing projects I left at home and the book I was writing. I mindlessly pull off the freeway for my daily latte and low-fat muffin. This is a nice diversion. It's a wonderful way to delay opening Dad's back door and entering into his world . . . because I know as soon as I do, only bad news will confront me.

"Mr. C slept through the rest of the night," Sam reports. "But today is not going very well. He's confused about where he is and what's going on around him. And he's beginning to 'stoke breathe.' The hospice nurse is with Mr. C right now. And she has increased the morphine patches."

I stand in the bedroom doorway and watch yet another horror movie unfold. Dad is refusing to take any substance, not even a sip of water. He is sure Sam is poisoning him. All the while he keeps trying to get out of bed. I understand now why Sam said some of her patients had to be in restrained near the end.

"My wife doesn't know where I am," Dad cries. "She'll kill me." *Where does he think he is right now? Whose bed is he trying to vacate?*

I can't enter his room. I can't bear to see him. I can only sit at the dining room table and work on another puzzle, hot tears rolling down my face. Every time I hear Dad's voice and Sam's calming reassurances, the tears increase. I can no longer control my emotional pain. *Oh God, please give Dad the peace he so deserves.*

David decides to spend the rest of the day in San Francisco. "I need to get out of this house," he tells me. "I don't feel I have a life anymore."

In the early afternoon, Dad begins to fight the Second World War. I can hear him yelling from his bedroom. Where is this coming from? What is he really trying to tell us? He was not involved in combat during the war, as a naval officer he spent it on the east coast. I can't escape the sound of his voice. I open a bottle of wine.

"Run. Take cover. Hurry, the bombs are coming!"

"I said, over here, down this path." He continues his frantic commands. "Arm yourselves, we are going to be wiped out!"

Occasionally he calls out to Mother . . .but not in a loving manner. He is either apologizing or escaping from what he feels will be a tongue lashing. He thrashes from side to side. Sam stays next to his bed to ensure he will not hurt himself. When will the increased dose of morphine take effect? I deliberately pour myself another glass of wine. I want dullness to take over my brain or for his voice to fade and become only a muddled sound in the background.

Someone knocks on the back door. Dad certainly doesn't need any visitors right now. Opening the door, I see a lady on the back stoop whom I have never seen before. She is large, around sixty, with tangled, dyed, fiery red hair.

"Are you going to be selling your father's car when he dies?" She greets me without introductions. I can't believe what this woman is asking. Her stance, and the strength of her voice let me know she thinks she is the one in charge here and she's used to getting her way.

"I'll pay cash for it," she continues in her matter of fact voice. "You decide on the price and let me know. Here, I have written down my name and number."

"But Dad isn't even dead yet."

"Yes." She shoves the piece of paper to me. "But I understand it won't be long now. Just give me a call as soon as you decide. I want to be first in line."

I am speechless and outraged at her insensitivity! Are there any more vultures out there planning to cross Dad's back steps? *I'll trash his car and send it over a cliff before I sell it to that bitch!*

* * *

Mary comes for her afternoon visit. She sits with me for a few minutes. Putting in some puzzle pieces, she musters up enough courage to drag herself into Dad's bedroom. The puzzle on the dining room table is the only working thread between us right now. She stands at his doorway for a moment, watching him sleep under the influence of morphine before going to his bedside. She holds his hand tenderly for only a few minutes, then walks down the hallway to the dining room.

"This is the last time," she says in a sad, but determined voice. "I can't do this anymore."

Bless her heart. I am amazed Mary has stuck it out so long. I only hope she is leaving with some happy memories. Memories of music and dancing on the ship around the Hawaiian Islands, the trip to Shasta and Lassen Park, the laughter, the warmth, and closeness of their friendship. I hope these will remain in her heart and not the struggle Dad has gone through to die. Neither of us speak as she quickly walks out the back door and down the steps to her car.

* * *

My brother arrives. He has brought some of his work, trying to catch up on the backlog. He concentrates, hoping to drown out the strange one-sided conversation sporadically erupting from Dad's bedroom. He only ventures as far as Dad's doorway, he can't go any farther.

Bill leaves late in the afternoon. I don't feel comfortable leaving just yet. I keep Sam company during supper and try to assess the situation.

I can't handle staying in Dad's room for more than a few brief moments. Not only is the smell unbearable; but the man in bed is not my father. This man must weigh all of 90 pounds. The swelling in his extremities, the gray skin, sunken cheeks, and the wide open mouth when sleeping; are not my father. It can't be *my* father. Clarence Compton is strong and powerful. He wouldn't let anything like this take him down.

At eight in the evening, I call Bill.

"Dad won't make it through this night. You and Kathy had better come on out here. Besides I can't stand being alone any longer."

It doesn't take more than 30 minutes for Bill and Kathy to arrive with popcorn, sleeping bags, and other necessities. We decide Dad's minister needs to be here as well. She arrives 45 minutes later. The four of us sit together in the living room. Sam stays with Dad. I am nursing another bottle of wine. I go through Dad's listening library of tapes and select a few I feel might be his favorites, ones I have heard often in his home. Sam again sets up her tape deck next to his bed. The soothing piano and organ melodies fill the house. But Dad complains he can't hear the music, it's too soft, he says, even though Sam has turned up the volume to its fullest.

The three of us take turns sitting on one side of Dad's bed. Sam is always on the other. He talks about seeing people who have passed on long ago gathered in his room. Every once in a while, he calls out to Mother again. Dad's breathing pattern is very irregular. His hands rest on his chest in an unnatural position as though they were no longer a part of his body. The little urine output he has is dark and thick. The end is very near, maybe only an hour more, Sam tells us.

I don't stay long when it is my turn to be with Dad. The smell of cancer is too overwhelming. Dad now has one eye closed. The other remains wide open and wanders around the room as if he is taking a journey somewhere far away. Each time he travels, he goes farther; taking longer trips during his unconscious periods.

I return to the living room. Bill and I have periodic laughing spells, reminiscing about funny times when we were children. We even laugh about some of the strange things Dad has done or said during the last couple of weeks. It is an emotional release. The laughter is much too long and loud to accompany the memory just recalled. But when the laughter vanishes the tears return. The minister holds our hands, prays, and works to come up with consoling words. She feels Dad has lingered so long because of the way he has lived his life. "He has always been on the go, so energetic, more life and energy than most people half his age—always, all wound up. It takes longer for someone like that to unwind and let go." I have heard that from hospice nurses as well.

We discuss the details of Dad's memorial service. Bill and I want to make sure the minister understands his wishes. She is quick to let us know, "A memorial service is for you as well as your father. It's for all his friends and family to remember and to grieve for their loss."

Funny, I hadn't put all that together before. I was only thinking about what Dad would want for *his* service. I like this, she's right; it is our service and our tribute to our father.

It doesn't look like he's leaving this world tonight after all. He is finally peacefully asleep. It's ten o'clock. The minister is exhausted, with the other church members who are in the final stages of cancer she is trying to be there for all three. The minister goes home to her family. Bill and Kathy leave around one in the morning, determined to get a few hours sleep. I remain on the sofa taking short naps between the every fifteen-minute chimes of the anniversary clock.

Tuesday, April 18th

After a few hours of uninterrupted sleep and a couple of cups of Sam's strong coffee, the vigil begins again. Bill arrives. "I just don't know where else to be today. I know I will be useless at work."

I have an appointment with the social worker from hospice at eleven. I like her and maybe she can help me drag myself through the last part of this ordeal. I am also going to get my hair cut. Something for me, a little pampering, a diversion. This should help.

Before leaving, I turn on Dad's computer. The daily emails to and from my husband have worked out very well. Without them our phone bills would probably have exceeded the state budget by now.

Joe tells me he has an appointment this morning to look over the house we will probably buy. We have to make a decision in the next two days. I recall the pictures he showed me when he was here, I also recall I wasn't very thrilled with them. He lets me know, "From now on, Leslie, I will keep my cell phone turned on and place it next to my pillow at night."

Wednesday, April 19

Before I can take my first sip of tea at Bill's, Sam calls. It's seven in the morning.

"Come as soon as possible. Mr. C is asking for you."

I pour my tea down the sink, rinse out my cup, and head for the door. No stopping today for my latte and muffin.

Quickly parking the car, I quietly tiptoe into Dad's bedroom, not sure of what to expect.

"Thank goodness you're here. Where have you been?" He seems relieved to see me. A wonderful warm feeling flows through my body. My father not only needs me, but he has actually asked for me. I can now sit with him, maybe help him relax, and relieve some of his fears.

This emotional high is quickly replaced with anxiety. Dad isn't seeing *me* standing next to his bed. He sees someone else in this room.

"Marian, thank you, I knew you would come to take care of me." He thinks I am Mother, his wife!

"Why are all the doctors in here?" Dad demands to know. There are no doctors or nurses in his room. He continues, "This room is full of people all gathered around my bed, all dressed in white. What are they doing here?" He's confused. He doesn't know why they have come to see him. He is upset that so many people have filled his room. "Tell these people to leave, *now!*" he yells at me.

Sam sits in Mother's chair next to Dad's bed. "Every time I sit in your mother's rocker I feel a cold breeze. Your mother is here to help your father," she tells me in a whisper.

I'm sure this room is full of his old friends and family waiting to help him cross over to the next life . . . waiting to welcome him with open arms.

I slip into the chair on the other side of the bed next to his hissing inflatable mattress and gently put his swollen hand into mine. His bloated fingers look very painful, so I am careful not to squeeze or to put any pressure. He breathes out a deep sigh. "Ah—finally." And closes his eyes.

Five minutes later, his eyes open and he asks, "How did they contact you? How did you know how to find me?"

"Dad, I'm your daughter, Leslie. Sam called me on the phone and told me to come over. She said you wanted to see me."

A confused look crosses his face. It's obvious, he can't quite put all that together.

"I have to make sure I get my fish." *Now where is he?*

"Of course, Dad. I'll make sure," I assure him. "I'll always make sure you get that fish, Dad."

A smile crosses my lips even in this dark moment. Daddy always loved to go fishing during our vacations at the beach. But there was that one summer…

> I was up before the dawn on that June morning in our vacation cottage at Newport Beach. I wanted to see if I could collect another bag of unusual shells during low tide. Maybe I could even find a whole sand dollar. I slipped on my sweatshirt and white shorts. Silently I tiptoed through the house, careful not to awaken the rest of the family. Daddy was also up early. He had decided to do some surf fishing. He put his index finger to his pursed lips to indicate that all would be okay if we just slip out the door quietly.
>
> Dad and his tackle box settled on the sandy shore. The surf was breaking on the beach. He always enjoyed the solitude of the early morning calm. He delighted in watching the

waves dance on the sand and listening to the sea gulls crying out overhead.

Daddy cast the line from his heavy surf pole out beyond the waves. Time after time he tugged and heaved at his pole, reeling it in, only to unhook long entangled vines of seaweed. I paid little attention. We each had our morning rituals; the quiet time before the rest of the world arrived with umbrellas, portable radios, and beach blankets. No matter how far I ventured from the cottage, I was always able to look back and see my father and his fishing pole standing close to shore.

And Daddy always wore his ugly, yellow, knit swim trunks. Those trunks must have been hand knit by someone in the early 40's using the first neon thread. They fit him like a second skin and revealed all of his private parts. At thirteen, I was thoroughly embarrassed! If he were on the Olympic swim team, he might have looked perfectly acceptable. But, at Newport Beach in 1955, correct fashion was all the rage. All other men were wearing swimsuits that resembled patterned boxer shorts. Why, even Mother and I had swimsuits with 'little boy shorts' attached. But Dad never seemed to care. "Heck," he would always say, "This suit fits me fine, has always fit me just fine. Why would I buy a new one when this one is perfectly okay?" Gad!

An hour or so later I headed back to our cottage with my garbage bag partially full of beautiful shells. In the distance I noticed Dad's fishing pole angled in a complete arch. "Good grief, what has he snagged, anyway?" I thought. "Surely not more seaweed!" I ran toward him through the wet sand. "Maybe this time——?" When I reached him his mouth was all screwed up as though his lips and tongue were reeling in a monster. No, not more seaweed. This thing on the end of his pole was huge! As he struggled to beach the monster, it began to look like something I remembered viewing through the glass windows of the San Francisco Aquarium.

"Leslie, Leslie, hurry! Run back and grab my camera, Quick!"

Hearing Dad's urgent request, I dropped my bag of shells and ran as quickly as I could to our cottage. Hurrying back to the beach with his Argus in tow, I realized he wanted me to take a picture of him. I had never been allowed to touch his camera, let alone focus and take a once in a lifetime photograph.

"Hurry", he said. "Hand me the camera, I'll set it up. You look into the lens and snap the shutter with this button."

He did some fancy finger work with the dials and handed it back to me. There he was for all to see, standing proudly in his tight, neon yellow swimsuit holding up a huge shovel-nosed shark. In his other hand he held the rod that had miraculously hooked this creature. His broad smile remained constant as I backed down the sandy incline to locate him and that fish in the viewfinder.

"Take it! Hurry up! I can't hold this thing much longer," I heard him yell through clenched teeth while still maintaining his photographic smile. With unsteady hands, I managed to push my right index finger and click the shutter.

What a wonderful fish tale Daddy was able to tell when he returned to work, accompanied by my photo to prove it.

* * *

I am quickly brought back to the present. Dad is fidgeting with his sheet. He tries to get out of bed to go to his 'wife.' He keeps repeating, "She doesn't know where I am. I must get to her." Dad begins to fight the war again. I leave the room. I drown out the sounds by working on my puzzle and doing my wash. I periodically go in and sit with him, bringing along a book. I am hopeful he will sleep so I can read. This struggle is just too difficult to watch. *Please just let go, Dad.*

Our regular nurse arrives for her daily visit. She increases his morphine patches once again. Hopefully this will settle him down a bit. She takes his temperature and reports that it is 99 degrees. I am not concerned with a low-grade fever, "But 99 degrees," she tells me, "indicates Clarence is now actively dying."

Actively Dying. I thought I was prepared for this announcement. In fact I have been praying for it. *I'm not ready.* I am a wreck. What a huge hole he is going to leave in my life. The emotional dam so fragilely held together, begins to split wide open. Tears cascade down my cheeks.

"Your father is to have nothing by mouth. It will only feed the cancer," the nurse tells me. "When he gets thirsty, use the lemon-flavored swabs I am leaving and swipe the inside of his mouth."

I open a bottle of wine. After all, it is one in the afternoon. Somewhere on this planet it must be cocktail hour. I'll just pretend I am there instead of here. *Work, damn it! Do your magic. Fuzz my brain into a non-feeling existence!*

"Leslie!" I am amazed Dad can still yell that loudly. I run back to his room.

"You must make that last phone call. It is almost five o'clock. Remember the electricity and phones shut down at five. Hurry up the hill; make that call. *Hurry!*"

I leave his room with the pretense of going to the telephone. I haven't a clue what he is talking about. Tears blur my vision.

Sam retrieves her Bible, claiming Dad wants the Psalms read

aloud. *(How the heck does she know?)* She holds his hand, recites the 23rd Psalm, and sings a hymn. It seems to soothe him and keeps him out of the War. He closes his eyes and begins to 'stoke breathe.'

Dad appears to be resting. It is dinnertime and I want to be at Bill's. All day I have been listening to Dad fight the Second World War. I gather up my needlepoint, my book that never seems to get finished, and my purse, for the drive back in commute traffic.

Bill's phone rings as we all prepare for bed. Sam reports, "Mr. C is throwing up again, dark green stuff. He is shaking like he is having convulsions." I phone hospice from Bill's. They call Sam.

"Give him twice his morphine, twice the medication for nausea, twice everything. In other words, just dope him out!" At two in the morning, Sam calls us again to report Dad's temperature has shot up to 103.6.

Thursday, April 20th

Arriving, I can see Dad looks like hell. Sam doesn't look a whole lot better; she never made it to bed last night. All night long she gave Dad Tylenol suppositories to bring down his temperature, more morphine in his cheek to sedate him, and placed cool wet washcloths on his face. But no matter what comfort measures Sam continually tries, Dad's temperature keeps rising.

I take his swollen, puffy hand in mine. This morning he knows who I am. After smiling his acknowledgment, he goes back to sleep. He can only close his eyes partway now, so I try not to look at him while he dozes. That smell is worse today, but at least we can open the windows to bring in the warm, spring breezes.

Since we know death is imminent and Dad can't last more than a few days, I call Bill and we decide on May 13th for Dad's memorial service. I make the necessary arrangements by phone. I need something to do that makes me feel functional and alive. The church, the minister, the piano player, and the caterer are all available. We then select May 6th to drive to the Sierras to spread his ashes. We'll rent a Town Car so his ashes can go in style like Mother's did. He will like that. We'll spread Dad's ashes in the same area where we scattered Mother's, where they had their honeymoon.

The telephone interrupts my planning. "Hello. Is this Leslie Compton?"

"Yes, who is this?"

"I live outside the park in San Leandro and my brother and his wife live in Grass Valley. They are getting too old to live so far away, so I told them to buy in this area to be closer to the rest of their family. They are here just for a couple of days. Can I drive them by to see your Dad's place? You won't mind if we come in, will you?"

I'll be damned! The vultures are striking again! But I don't want to refuse them. It would be a lot easier to sell the place outright instead of putting it on the market, paying a real estate agent, and forking out the monthly space rental fee for God knows how long. But does it have to be right now?

"You know my father is dying even as we speak? Can you wait a couple of days?"

"Oh, that's okay with us, just close his door, we won't disturb him. *Where the hell did this brassy person come from?* "We just want to see the inside of the place."

Reluctantly, I agree. I quickly begin picking up the odds and ends I have left around the house and run the vacuum. We open all the windows and Sam sprays air fresheners everywhere, hoping to neutralize 'The Smell.' We close Dad's door. *Good grief, people can't even die around here before they are on us like flies.* But hey, they want to come in and see this place looking like a wreck and pay cash without demanding any repairs? Have at it!

I am shocked when I look in the mirror. My eyes are red, swollen, and puffy. *Seems to be the normal state of affairs lately. Oh, well, these people are not coming to buy me; they are coming to view the property.*

Fifteen minutes later the front doorbell announces our visitors. "Everyone in their places!" Sam yells and retreats quickly to Dad's room. Before closing Dad's door she adds, "If I get a glimpse of these brazen people, I will let them have a piece of my mind!" *These are prospective buyers, I keep telling myself; smile now.*

The caller pushes her way through the front door before I have it fully opened. Quickly introducing herself and her relatives, she whisks them through the other rooms of the house, all the while convincing them this is the mobile home to buy. I have to keep remembering to close my mouth; I find it dropping open periodically in amazement while watching the circus being performed right in front of me.

"Where does that door lead to?" the prospective buyer asks. I open my mouth to explain about the closed door at the end of hall, but behind her brother's back, the caller shakes her head and puts her index finger to her lips. *My God, she hasn't told these people what is going on this house?*

"My father is ill and doesn't want to be disturbed right now." I force a smile, having trouble controlling my anger. *Come back in a couple of days, he'll be good as new. Why, he'll probably want to take you on a tour himself!*

They ask to see the storage sheds along the carport. I can't show them, for I have lost both the keys, not a good thing. We'll have to jimmy them open later. I've also lost $200 of Dad's. I know I put it somewhere. Mother's comment would be, "You'd probably lose your head if it were not attached." She would undoubtedly be right.

Within thirty minutes they decide they want to buy the place and promise to return soon. *I'll be damned!*

Before I explode, I let Sam know I need to take a break and go to the grocery store. I load up the shopping cart with fun foods, easy to fix meals, and tasty treats for Sam. The last two days she has only been snacking and hasn't had time to cook anything for herself.

Bill arrives. We work on Dad's obituary and the invitation to his memorial service. We want it all to be so special, a real celebration of his life. We want Dad to be pleased that we are carrying out his wishes for his service.

Returning to Oakland, I find Kathy reluctantly making preparations to go to her niece's wedding in Southern California during this Easter weekend. Both Bill and I encourage her to make this trip with her family. She needs to get away. What more can she do here? Bill doesn't want to go to the wedding as previously planned. He doesn't want to leave Dad. We finally all head for bed. Once again exhausted, but unable to sleep . . . anticipating that last phone call.

Friday, April 21

I can't bear to sit with Daddy for long periods of time. I look in on him only once in a while just to let him know I am still here. I watch his chest rise and fall when he takes a breath and listen to the gurgle sound that follows.

"It's okay, Dad. You can go now. Bill and I have it all under control. Your vegetables and roses look beautiful." I talk softly to him. "You did a good job of directing. Everything is in place. I love you, Daddy."

I can see by his flickering eyelids he can hear me. I am no longer able to endure. I leave his bedside, feeling very guilty, I huddle in the living room without music or TV for fear I might disturb him. I feel like I have let my father down. I am not there for him; I promised I would be.

"You'll be there for me, won't you?" Our earlier conversation echoes in my head.

"Of course, Dad. You know I will."

Even Sam with all her experience caring for hospice patients can't believe how long Mr. C has prolonged his death. She is now giving him morphine every hour.

"Forget charting down the meds, just dope him up and make him comfortable," I tell her. She nods her agreement.

But no matter how much painkiller is given, Dad remains with us. My poor father. He didn't want to go this way. Last summer he asked me to make his death happen quickly. He wanted me to give him extra doses of morphine to take him out when the cancer got bad. Thank goodness that conversation has not been mentioned again.

I settle in the family room and begin making more calls to arrange for his memorial service. Dad wants the luncheon to be at the clubhouse. There are only a few available parking spaces. The other parking areas are located on different streets. Many of the people who will be attending the luncheon won't be able to walk very far. *We*, the mourners, will have to take care of parking cars and driving friends and family to the door of the clubhouse. *We*, the mourners, will have to set up the tables for the luncheon, and *We*, the mourners, will have to take them down and sweep the floor. No wonder most people leave the details for a mortuary to handle.

David says goodbye to his grandfather and tells him how much he loves him. I am so proud of that young man. Dad acknowledges him with a smile. It's time for David to leave. There is nothing more he can do. Just being here has taken a toll on him; his exhaustion is visible all over his face. I take David to the airport, so grateful he has been able to put his life on hold for such a long time. I will miss my son's loving support.

Our hospice nurse arrives in the afternoon. I have come to adore this lady. She continues to bring all of us comfort with each visit. She spends time with Dad, softly speaking to him. She gently covers his hand with the two of hers. "I won't be seeing you again, Clarence, because this is Friday and I have the weekend off. I wish you a wonderful journey forward. It has been such a pleasure and an honor to have known you."

I stand in the doorway crying softly. I am amazed that there are any tears left. The nurse gives me a hug and whispers, "just make him as comfortable as possible."

Sam and I return to the kitchen to eat comfort food and drink coffee. Try to keep our minds off of Dad.

Late that evening, I drag myself back to Bill's. Kathy finally gave in and has left for her Southern California wedding. My brother and I are alone. It seems appropriate. It'll be just the two of us who will receive tonight's anticipated phone call. *"It's okay, Dad. Please let go,"* I say to myself over and over, hoping he can hear me, hoping he finally believes we really do have things under control. After all, the best control person around taught us how to handle details and get things accomplished.

Bill and I settle in for the night and are convinced we will be awakened in a few short hours. He sleeps fitfully, afraid his beeper will scare him to death when it sounds its alarm. I sleep very deeply until three o'clock when I awake with all the details of Dad's service racing through my head. I never do get back to sleep.

Saturday, April 22nd

Bill and I have decided that from now on we are visiting Dad together. We can't do it alone any more. We need each other's support. Today, when we peek into Dad's room, Sam's sitting next to him in the rocking chair. She has spent the night there, administering suppositories and squirting morphine into his cheek every hour. She has also bathed him, changed his position, sang hymns, and read aloud to him from her Bible. *My God, where did this angel come from?*

Dad tries to speak but we can't understand him. It seems he feels something is not finished, something he wants us to accomplish before he leaves this world.

An unfamiliar hospice nurse arrives in the afternoon. Dad's temperature hovers around 102 and, with each breath, a rattle follows. Sam ordered a suction machine. It seems to help some, but not enough to relieve the rattle. Dad occasionally tries to cough up phlegm, but he can't produce anything effective. The nurse orders a new patch to help dry up the mucus. He tells us Dad's heartbeat and breathing indicates the end is soon.

I return to Dad's room after the nurse leaves. What little energy I had when I arrived this morning has now vanished. I feel limp, like a wet, moldy washrag.

It is seven in the evening. I jot a quick email to my husband. This has become a ritual. I look forward each evening to connecting with Joe. "No change in Dad," I write. "He remained the same all day."

Bill and I head back to Oakland. I make a crab salad and he rents a movie; one we can both laugh at, forgetting the world around us. We are glad to be together, just the two of us . . . Dad's two children.

Sam tries again to control Dad's rising temperature most of the night. By two AM it reaches 103.6. He coughs up dried blood. She suctions him. He coughs up black and green mucus. She gives him morphine and suppositories and wraps him in cool towels. She freezes water in plastic bags and puts ice into water bottles. Placing one under each of Dad's armpits and one under each knee, she helps bring down his temperature. By six o'clock he finally calms down a little and rests on his left side.

Easter Sunday, April 23rd

Last night, I slept better than I have in weeks. I awake feeling very rested. I vacuum Bill's house, spend time reading, drinking tea, and washing my hair. I feel full of energy and life this morning, how unusual. The sun is shining brightly—it's Easter. A wonderful day.

I drive to Lake Chabot for a walk and enjoy watching families spread colorful tablecloths over redwood picnic tables and bring food baskets from their cars, preparing for Easter dinner. The ducks and geese swim close to shore, hoping for handouts. Wildflowers are in bloom. Birds everywhere are singing. It is a beautiful day.

Bill and I drive to Dad's around noon. No need to go any earlier. I don't think Dad knows the difference at this point. Bill brings some work to do. He is becoming further behind with his clients.

To our surprise we find Dad's breathing is fairly normal and he even recognizes me when I go to his bedside. Dad's temperature registers 104.5. Sam continues the iced water bottles to keep him cool. She covers his face with cold, wet washcloths and leaves him uncovered. Dad can't form his words, but attempts to tell me something. He can't make himself understood, but he is able to let me know with a smile, he's glad I am here.

I work in Dad's yard for a while, pulling the weeds that have dared to show themselves, and water the thriving new plants, things David had been doing. The warm healing sun feels good on my back. I work on a needlepoint project later in the day as my jigsaw puzzle stock has run dry.

I eagerly turn on Dad's computer to read the daily message from my husband. Joe keeps a candle lit for Dad. He loves my father. "I have such a sadness in my chest…a mix of feelings your dad leaves me…the loss of his vibrancy and the support he gave me and a melancholy rerun of my personal videotape of special moments I had with him. At the evening fire in the campground, working together on projects, sharpening his knife, huffing off to get something done that wasn't happening fast enough, every physical move a practical 'hands on' action to get things done." The tears freely run down my face as I read my husband's words. They say so much of how we all feel about the man in the next room suspended between life and death.

The same hospice nurse from yesterday arrives. Dad actually recognizes him, smiles, and whispers, "Hi." Dad's temperature is down to 101.5. *I know it is Easter Sunday, but give me a break. Dad is not rising from the dead today. I won't be able to handle that one. Why is he hanging on? What is it he feels he has yet to accomplish?*

What else can I say to my father that hasn't already been said? I know I may feel guilty when this is over, anguish that I should have stayed with him more. Regrets, because I should have been able to put my feelings aside, and remorse that I didn't do more to make him comfortable. At the same time, I wonder what more I could have done?

The day wears on. Dad's temperature drops as his body begins to cool. His breathing slows down again. Sam continues to give him hourly pain medications. By five PM his temperature slips down to 100.4. Sam remains in his room tending to his every need.

Daddy appears to be resting now. His breathing is regular again, accompanied by gurgling sounds. He no longer closes his eyes, but stares at the ceiling. His mouth does not close. His feet are turning blue. Somehow he reminds me of those skeletons I often see displayed in science classrooms.

"Daddy, please let go," I whisper softly. "Please go to the bright light. Go to your friends and family who are waiting. This body is of no more use to you." He responds with the raising of an eyebrow and a slight twitch of the corner of his mouth. But I know he will do things *his* way, he always has. "Goodbye, Daddy. I love you," I tell him softly. "I'll see you tomorrow." But as I back out of the room, I have a pulling feeling that's telling me I should stay here and not go back with my brother.

Bill takes his turn telling Dad goodbye. It is difficult for either of us to linger with him for very long. I know the image of his misshapen, gaunt body will live with us long after his death. Bill and I leave for Oakland, not sure we are doing the right thing.

Very shortly after we arrive at Bill's, Kathy pulls into the garage. She is very tired after her long drive from Southern California, but relieved to be home. She shares with us the festivities of the wedding. We share with her the downhill spiral our father is having with death.

"Should I call my teaching partner to say I won't be in to work tomorrow? Shouldn't I stay here with you two?"

I suggest she call Sam for an update before she makes that decision.

Sam gives her report. "Mr. C is still hanging in there. He is still the same, no change either way." Kathy puts the phone down and looks up her partner's number.

"I just don't feel right about going to work," she relays to us.

At eight-fifteen, she dials her partner. At eight-sixteen, Bill's pager fills the room with its ugly, loud, "beep, beep, beep." No one moves. Our feet are frozen in place. We are standing in the dining area. There is total silence. Instantly we know. I feel myself sway, feeling the flood of grief filling my aching heart. Kathy is the first to gain some composure. She blurts into the receiver, "I won't be at work tomorrow," and hangs up. Bill pulls his pager from its hook on his pants pocket and looks at the read-out, 911. It's the message we agreed upon—Dad is dead.

We three stare at the pager's printout, not moving and hoping there was a mistake. And yet, we feel the whole significance of its reality. If we just stand here together, everything will be okay. Somehow, as long as we don't move, stay this way forever, we can stop time, and this moment won't ever have happened. Instantly it'll all go away. These last few months will only have been a bad dream.

* * *

Bill is the first to move. He picks up the phone and calls Sam.

"Mr. C left for his long journey home. I had been with him all afternoon and as soon as I stepped out of the room, he died. I haven't called the Neptune Society yet. I didn't know if you wanted to see him before they took him away."

"We'll be right there," he responds.

We do and we don't want to go. But we all pile into Kathy's

still-warm station wagon for the ride to Hayward. Daddy waited until his daughter-in-law returned from her trip. He knew we needed her extra support. He knew we needed to be together. Sitting in the back seat, I think of the comment Dad made fourteen days ago. "I'm going to stick around for another two weeks."

His house is silent. The oxygen has been turned off, and the rattled breathing has ceased. Sam warns us that she was unable to close Dad's eyes or mouth as she had wished. But she has washed him and taken the oxygen from his nose.

I enter Dad's room with trepidation. The only sound is the constant 'breathing' of the bed circulating its air through the five sections of plastic. Dad isn't there. In his place is a small, skeletal body, its jaw dropped down, eyes glassy, still staring at the ceiling. Perhaps he was looking upward, seeing people and angels all around him. I don't feel his spirit anywhere. I wanted to feel his presence as he moved forward to the next life. I thought that would be comforting. I wonder why he didn't go when I was with him. Did he feel I couldn't handle it? But maybe Dad didn't want to linger any longer, he just needed to get on with it, because after all; "That's just the way life is."

I leave quickly, not wanting to touch the gnarled hands that Sam has tried to fold over his chest. Bill views the body from the safety of the doorway. Neptune Society is called. It's Easter Sunday, but they still tell us they'll be here within the hour.

The four of us sit staring at each other in the living room. We wait for them to arrive and take Dad away. Sam is exhausted. How she was able to tend to Dad's every need and still be here for us is amazing. She has been such a blessing.

Out of the corner of my eye I see the lights of the white wagon as it pulls up to the curb. "I have to run, *now*!" I loudly announce. "I have to get out of here. I can't see them take Daddy away forever."

Kathy follows me out the back door. We walk long into the night, winding through the streets of the mobile home park. The faster I walk, the harder I cry. "My father is dead, goddamn it! Don't take my Daddy away from me!" I scream. I don't have to hide my sobs anymore, and I don't care who hears me. Let me wake up all the residents and have them rush to their windows. My brother married a very special lady. Kathy lets me yell and sob until I feel as though my whole body is crumbling.

Bill waits inside Dad's home, signing the necessary paperwork. Hours seem to pass. Or has it been only a few minutes? Kathy and I return to Dad's home. The white wagon has gone. She drives us back to their house around two in the morning, the only one capable of operating a car right now. There is only silence. There is nothing left that needs to be said.

Monday, April 24th

The sun flows through the window next to my inflatable mattress onto Bill's living room floor. The vertical blinds are rattling gently with an early morning breeze. It's six o'clock, a Monday, the beginning of a work week. I hear commute traffic in the distance. Life is going on as usual. I am sure the same people will be congregating in my coffee shop before they begin their day. They will converse with one another about their outings on Easter Sunday. It feels amazing to me that life is still going on around me. Everyone is driving in the same car down the same highway, going to the same job, wearing the same clothes, having the same breakfast—and—*my father is dead.*

I can't sleep any longer. Every muscle, every bone in my body feels crushed . . . as though run over by a sixteen-wheeler. I am sure it will be a while before this feeling goes away. I shower and dress, moving in a daze. I look at myself in the mirror and hardly recognize the image that reflects back to me. Somewhere in a deep, dark place in my soul, I must have thought that if I just sacrificed enough, I could keep Daddy alive. All the time, energy, and money I've spent in the last few years and all I have to show for it is a worn out body and mind—Daddy and Mother died anyway. *Did it matter whether I was there for them?*

Bill and I have an appointment with the Neptune Society this morning. Our parents prepaid for their cremation years ago.

We are welcomed into a nicely furnished waiting room with thick, plush carpet, walnut paneling, soft music playing in the background. Green, healthy plants decorate the end tables and a tall ficus tree fills the corner. We are the only people here. I am sure it has been planned this way.

After only a short wait we are greeted by a young woman dressed in a business suit and heels. She ushers us into a private room where we're asked to sit in comfortable, overstuffed chairs facing another woman seated at a desk. Our greeter leaves. After the introductions, the lady behind the desk excuses herself, promising to return shortly. All around the room are decorative shelves created from expensive woods. They display urns of varying sizes, qualities, and materials looking like collectible Russian eggs or exquisite French porcelain. Next to each container, is a very discreetly placed price tag. No other decorations are in the room.

It takes only a couple of minutes for both Bill and I to realize what's going on. I am sure the room is bugged. *"We are not here to buy an expensive urn for our father's ashes to sit on our mantel for all time!"* I loudly exclaim. Bill and I make jokes about their fancy price stickers and talk about how disgusted we are with this underhanded sell job. Within minutes after a few of these negatives remarks, the lady behind the desk returns.

We sign the papers to have Dad cremated. "No," we say. "We don't want to view him again." And, "No, we don't want to watch him through a window as he is cremated!"

As part of their service, Neptune Society will notify Social Security. Bill writes them a check from Dad's account for the transportation last night from the house to their 'holding tank.'

THAT'S JUST THE WAY LIFE IS...

Added to that expense is Dad's ride to the morgue this morning, the state taxes, the cardboard box for his cremation, and $79.00 for the simplest of containers to hold his remains. The lady tells us we can pick up his ashes by the end of the week. We are given papers, each one stamped with the same number. This is now Dad's number. He no longer will be known as Clarence Compton. Throughout today's ordeal, Dad's name was never mentioned. Mortuaries, like any other business, exist to make money.

Bill and I need a break and take a drive to Berkeley. I purchase different kinds of incense from street vendors, and $100 worth of CDs, all with upbeat music. I want to light incense in every room of Dad's house, to eliminate the cancer smell that still lingers. I want to play my loud, happy music to create new energy.

Returning to Dad's home, we put our purchases on the counter in Dad's kitchen and greet Sam. Immediately the phone rings. It's the outrageously outspoken woman whose relatives want to buy Dad's home!

"My brother made a special trip from Grass Valley just to see your Dad's house again. Can we come over in about half an hour?"

I can hardly contain my anger. "Sure, I'll be here." *What the hell.*

The party of three arrives precisely thirty minutes later.

"My condolences about your Dad." The woman brushes past me through the door. "But it was for the best." *How the hell does she know what is best for everyone in our family?*

I haven't been able to go into Dad's bedroom yet. I can only peer into his room from the doorway. The hospice bed is still there, its motor turned off. The mattress is flat and deflated. The oxygen tank sits by the window. Other equipment that hospice ordered is scattered around the room. I can't go in until that bed is gone. There is something so awful about seeing that bed all deflated with no one on it—I can't handle it right now.

As the prospective buyers head toward the bedroom, I tell their bitchy escort that I can't go in there with them. Dad just died in that room.

"Shhhh, shhh, be quiet," she whispers without shame. "Don't tell them your father died in this house!" *God forbid!* Sam picks up the clue and leads the couple through a tour of the master bedroom and bathroom. *Surely, they are not blind. Can't they figure out what is going on for themselves?*

After they complete their inside tour, I take all three of them to the back yard. I proudly point out the thriving vegetable garden, the healthy roses, and the producing lemon tree. Dad was so proud of his yard. But they seem unimpressed. The woman's next comment leaves me totally speechless!

"My brother and sister-in-law like this place. We'll be back on the 8th of May to make final arrangements. You'll be through with your grieving by then."

I can see and feel Dad at work here. He is making things happen *his* way. "Let's get things done now, it is time to move on." If it wasn't so important that Bill and I sell this place as fast as possible, I would have slapped her face!

* * *

I now need to face the task of notifying Dad's friends and relatives. It will take more than incense to get me through this afternoon. Sam offers to help. Bill and I have asked her to live here for a while longer. We still need her, and it's essential she take a break before her next patient. We take turns, thumbing through Dad's numerous address books and lists of clubs and organizations. I begin telephoning, working in slow motion, amazed my voice doesn't sound like a 78 record being played at 33-1/3 speed. The rest of my body certainly feels that way.

Tuesday, April 25

Today I will begin cleaning out Dad's house. Bill remains home, trying to catch up on some of his work that has piled up the last few days. The many books I have read state that a grieving person should have a brief intermission before selling a home, and/or weeding out belongings after a loved one has died. I don't have time for that breathing space. I also read recently that grief is inevitable, but so is survival. At this point I am not convinced about the survival part.

When I arrive at Dad's home, I find the bed and medical equipment have all been removed. What a relief! His bedroom now looks like just another room. I place my new CDs in Sam's boom box and turn up the volume. I light incense, beat my feet, and clap my hands to the music.

Two emotions hit me as I begin sorting through Dad's personal belongings. Because I love history and am a collector of old treasures, part of the searching and unveiling of the hidden secrets is a little exciting. On the other hand, so much of this chore is sad. Here are the wild and colorful shirts he purchased to celebrate his 85th birthday on the Hawaiian cruise with Mary. Here is the very expensive tie I bought him for the formal night aboard ship. And in this small, hand carved box is a single cuff link that belonged to his father, my grandfather. I touch these items; I want to feel Dad's energy again. But this place feels lifeless. One more time I am hit with the realization; Dad doesn't live here anymore.

I designate one corner of his bedroom for trash, one for Goodwill, one for sale items, and one for us to think about. Sam stays in the bedroom with me. She doesn't want me to be alone. She still wants to protect and care for someone. But I want to be alone to grieve and to sense my father again. I want to experience the feeling he had for each and every item I pick up. I can't do that in Sam's presence. She continues babbling, throwing in light-hearted jokes every few sentences, I guess trying to make this day bright and cheery. I don't want to be bright and cheery. I need to have it be okay to experience any emotion that may tug at my heart.

The windows are open, the blinds are raised, and warm sunshine pours into the room. Music is turned up so loud, I have to yell to make myself heard. Slowly Dad's room begins to change shape. The items left don't look the same to me anymore. Nothing is as it was. It is as though this house was just a detour on Dad's journey through his life, lingering here for just a short while before moving on.

Kathy comes to help in the afternoon. We are not in good harmony today. I tend to react like my father . . . one goal in mind; buckle down, get the job done, and move on. She wants to take her time. She fondles each object, feels the texture, smells the familiar scent, remembering, commenting; sometimes letting a tear trickle down her cheek.

"Kathy, we don't have endless amounts of time to get this job done. If you want one of the items, just take it with you. I have a job to do today, let's get with the program!"

"Leslie, you are taking things much too quickly. You'll make yourself sick."

"She's absolutely right," chimes in Sam. "You need to slow down and take time to grieve."

Why does everyone have to follow a prescribed way of doing things? Who set down this *list of rules? I am doing what I do best, and for the first time in months I am feeling worthwhile, I am finally able to* accomplish *something! Everyone has their own way of grieving.*

As the day draws to a close, I have to admit, I am overwhelmed with all this 'stuff' around me. I'm 'also getting frazzled with all the 'help' and suggestions I am receiving. Seeing my frustration, Kathy tells me, "Well Leslie, you can always leave and go home; you don't have to stay and sort through this house. You have accomplished what you came here to do. We can just hire someone to come and take all of Dad's stuff away to the Goodwill or wherever and be done with it," "she declares.

"But I can't do that. What's here belongs to me too. I want some of Dad's treasures, some of the furniture, the books, some pictures, I want some memories."

Bill and I are having no problem dividing. We've already

discussed the placement of most of the folks' personal possessions. Years ago, we decided to not let 'things' come between us. Returning to Bill's house, he agrees with his wife. "We just can't go through all of Dad's stuff right now . . . We plan on taking a long time sorting through the items when we do."

"I don't have that option," I yell. "I want to go home but not before my job is completed." They both repeat, "You can go home now. We'll just hire someone to toss everything out. Nothing is that important."

There is a part of me that would just love to cash it all in and hand everything over to Bill and Kathy. But like my Dad, I am driven to complete what I have started.

"All well and good. But don't forget there is a buyer for Dad's house out in the wings who wants to move in June first. We have to set aside a weekend for a garage sale and probably another weekend for the flea market. We can't organize those two events until everything is sorted," I adamantly respond.

* * *

Days and weeks are now filled with sorting, packing, dragging garbage bags to the Goodwill and carting boxes to Bill's. They will go through them at a later time. I clean the house. I make phone calls. I meet with the minister, the Clubhouse director, the caterer; we have a memorial service to plan.

Cleaning the house has become a highly charged emotional chore. The refrigerator monster is full of subtle memories. It would've been better to have left it sealed and have it carted out to the dump. Cautiously I open the door to find the half full salsa jar Dad used every Sunday for his 'Mexican Omelet' and the different sauces he liked when he prepared his meals. I remove each jar, open the lid and smell it before I flush the contents down the toilet. I savor the memory of his bar-be-cue cooking; remembering the aroma from those meals, the marinated steaks, the legs of lamb. The salad dressings are next. Here is Mary's favorite. It's next to Dad's. Way back on the top shelf, is Dad's jug of water. Dad filled that plastic container each night with tap water to be cold and ready for him in the morning. The last things to throw out are two half empty ketchup bottles. Dad's garbage disposal has never been something I could count on, so I visit the toilet. I watch the red thick ooze gush out of the ketchup bottles onto the white porcelain. It coagulates as the glob slides down. It seems like the red river resembles my insides, being torn and ripped apart then poured out into the sewer. Slowly, slowly, it all descends to become one with the water and is flushed away. How profound! I can finally see what I have been feeling for so long being played out over the toilet bowl.

It feels like scavengers are descending on this house in droves. They bang on the door, hoping to be the first with their requests. Those that can't come to the house keep the phone ringing in the kitchen. "Can we have the bookcase by the dining room?" "How much are you asking for the TV?" "When are you selling the car? I want that car, it's 'still pretty new, isn't it?" Slowly, the items that were once meaningful to Dad and Mom begin to disappear. One by one, they are taken by strangers.

Those who've waited too long for their chance at a bargain angrily shout at me. Foul words are hurled my way because a relative has taken an item some stranger wanted to own. I am living *Zorba the Greek*. By the time the vultures leave carrying Dad's precious possessions under their arms, I begin shaking as though I have just consumed ten cups of coffee. These people have come like the cancer before them, eating all that represented my father. He held it all together. Now only a shell remains. It bears no resemblance to the structure my father once called home.

How can I explain the feeling of dismantling my father's things? Some of the items so personal are the items no one wanted. The cufflinks Dad wore when he worked at Capwell's. His photographic slide presentations. His projector. His tape deck and the contraption he created to operate the whole slide show. It's all in the garbage. No one wanted those items. The last of his dark room equipment. Unused film and bulbs ready for his next photo shoot. Mom's needlepoint stretcher bars, the wool scarves to keep Dad's neck warm in the winter, the space heater that warmed his bathroom on cold mornings. Mom's outdated Samsonite make-up case she always took with her in their motor home. No one wants those items.

* * *

It's warm in the kitchen and I still have cleaning to do. I plug in Dad's huge fan, anticipating a cool breeze on my back. Sparks fly and it moans loudly, screeches, and after forty years, dies. Dad doesn't need it anymore. It goes on the dump pile. The back porch light, left on 24 hours a day for security reasons, burned out last night. Some of Daddy's tomato plants are dying and I can't do anything about them. The beautiful blooming roses have all faded and wilted. The doves have matured and outgrown their nest over Dad's front door. They took flight this morning. Everything is gone. Dad doesn't live here anymore, he has a new address.

One day flows into another; becomes the other. Each evening when I return to Bill and Kathy's, their hallway is filled with more boxes. Some stacks reach the ceiling. We have decided on a compromise. Later in the summer they will go through these boxes and decide in their own time what they want to do with the contents.

May

Final Thought

What we bury here today
Is the outward robe of clay.
But the flesh that fought in vain,
'Gainst Life's never-ending strain.
All that fretted him is gone.
All we loved in him lives on.

At the grave where now we grieve,
All that erred and failed we leave.
Like a coat that can't be matched,
Grown too threadbare to be patched,
Though he viewed it once with pride,
Now the flesh is put aside.

Sleeping? Yes, to wake again,
Done with suffering and pain;
Wake, to wear with greater ease
Longer, lasting robes than these.
This the body was the thing
Which contrived his suffering.

What we loved in him shall be
Glowing still in memory.
Here we place forevermore
Every hurt and pain he bore;
Nothing else from life has gone;
All we loved in him lives on.

—Edgar A. Guest
*(From Mother's college collection
of her favorite poems)*

Saturday, May 6

Joe arrived late last night; we're staying at a local motel. Around eight this morning, we drive to Bill's in the Lincoln Town Car we've rented.

Bill and Kathy are ready for us. They carry backpacks, walking shoes, water bottles, and Bill carries the black box containing Dad's ashes. The box is enclosed in a purple velvet bag with gold-corded drawstrings. Bill puts the purple bag into his backpack so we look like hikers rather than mourners. This is not out of disrespect, but because the location my parents selected to have their ashes distributed is no longer private property. PG&E now owns it, using it for water shed. Angry dark clouds have filled the sky, promising to drench us. Joe drives. Bill sits in the front passenger seat, his backpack strapped with the seat belt in the middle. This is how we planned it, just like Mother's last ride.

It's a four-hour drive to the area where Mom and Dad spent their honeymoon, and many happy weekends later on. There's very little conversation in the car. Everything has already been said. Bill and I silently rehearse the parts of the service we have separately planned.

When we reach our destination, we park in a turnout and continue our journey on foot. The four of us hike about 45 minutes along the PG&E water ditch to the grove of cypress trees. Bill and I recall stories our folks told us about swimming in that ditch, and about camping at the log cabin built by Mom's father. We hike deeper into the forest, hoping the swollen clouds will keep their floodgates closed for a little while longer.

The grove is easy to spot from a distance. We were just here three years ago. Bill reads some passages from *A Conversation with God*. I read "Death" from the *Prophet*; the same book Dad carried with him during World War II. I also read the 23rd psalm and some passages from the old version of the *Episcopal Book of Common Prayer*. Bill takes the purple bag from his backpack. He retrieves the box from inside. Just as he opens the container, an unexpected breeze comes over the grove, picking up the ashes, scattering them throughout the forest. Just the way Dad would want it.

"Ashes to ashes, dust to dust." It is over.

* * *

Epilogue

Wednesday, May 17

Dad is gone, and along with him, a part of me is gone. Joe is flying back to Massachusetts.

It's a cool morning. The summer fog is lifting. I have reserved a wonderful hotel room in Berkeley, on the San Francisco Bay, just for me. I need time to be by myself before the trip home to Boston. I walk the paths around the Marina. It is so peaceful. I listen to and watch red-wing black birds protecting their nests hidden in wild grasses. Each male sits on a twig a few feet from the next one down the line. They spread their wings to show red tipped feathers, stating to everyone and everything within earshot, "My territory, my territory!"

I pause on a worn wooden bench and listen to the birds. I watch small waves wash the shore. Last Saturday was Dad's memorial service. It seems a blur, but sitting here, I try to put the pieces together, listening to the rhythmic motion of the water splashing on nearby rocks.

One of Dad's requests was to have his memorial service include a nature slide show he'd created and shown around the Bay Area. Two projectors had to be used, timed so that one picture would fade into the next. Dad also created the cassette that narrated the show. Bill and Joe practiced for a couple of days to get everything in sync. Another tape recorder was set up to play music Dad especially enjoyed. This was Dad's memorial service, a celebration of his life.

Dad's minister spoke about the short time she had known him. Then it was my turn. This was the last time a room full of people would gather for my father. This was the last time I could stand in front of a large group and shout from the highest rafters what my father meant to me. I welcomed the opportunity.

Biting down the urge to cry, I took several short breaths and began.

Who was my father?

As a child I saw him as a builder of my toys, a swing, a slide, and a covered wagon created from scraps of lumber and a tired tricycle. I saw him as a carpenter, building garages, patios, and all my bedroom furniture, as well as most of the furnishings for our entire house.

I watched him go to Navy Reserve meetings dressed smartly in his officer's uniform, to woodshop classes to make use of tools he did not own, and to folk dancing classes with Mom.

As a child, I saw him as the Senior Warden for a new and thriving Episcopal Church in El Cerrito; singing tenor in the choir; involved in work parties; painting and gardening; always volunteering for jobs. If something needed to be done, just ask Clarence.

Even as a child I knew him as the keeper of the camera. The photographer of the family. His Argus housed in the worn brown leather case hung around his neck, replacing his tie and suit, regularly. I watched him constantly devour books, always stretching his mind and his imagination, never fully satisfying his thirst for learning.

But who was Mr. Compton?

As a child and young adult, I knew him as a high-powered executive at the Emporium-Capwell Company. I used to love to go shopping and watch the expression on a sales clerk's face when I flashed my charge card imprinted with C. E. Compton. Nothing was too good for Mr. Compton's daughter from that moment to the end of the transaction.

As a young adult I knew him on Christmas Eve, when he was the bearer of the largest selection of gorgeous packages I have yet to see duplicated. After all, Capwell's wrapped them all especially for Mr. Compton. And Christmas was also a time when I witnessed my father as the once-a-year violinist sawing his way through the carols while mother played the piano or the organ.

As a young adult, I saw the love he had for dancing and singing. I witnessed his performances at functions for church or at Capwell's parties, plucking away on the string bass, to the shock and amazement of the bass player in the band, or kicking up his heels to do his famous Balboa Hop. I never could keep up with him on the dance floor, though he gave me many opportunities to try.

But even as a young person, I also knew him as a very goal-orientated man, sometimes lacking patience for those who structured their lives differently than he did. I experienced him as undemonstrative, showing little or no affection for those close to him; always keeping deep feelings to himself.

So, who was Clarence?

As an adult, I was privileged to catch a glimpse of him as a grandfather creating a variety of paper airplanes that he and David sailed through the house . . . leaving behind rubber bands, paper clips, a ream of paper, and a very delighted child.

And as an adult, I was able to witness a very industrious, self-motivated individual. After retiring at the age of 55, he created a successful photography business, buying equipment and building a full color and black and white dark room in his home. And of course he was successful. Clarence wouldn't have it any other way. When he lost his retirement investments, thus plummeting his income to near poverty level, he just worked harder and longer in his dark room, creating more avenues for his pictures. "That's just the way life is," he said.

But then as a mature adult, I was finally privileged to get a small inkling into this man and to experience my father. It was in his later years when all of his responsibilities had been lifted from his shoulders that I watched him learn to love again; this time more openly, more fully. I heard his familiar chuckle develop into a new full-bodied laugh, and to sense his strong, determined zest for life. It was during these last years that I was privileged to see him smile and trudge on through the toughest of adversities. And I experienced and watched his reaching out with hugs and kisses and with whispers of "I love you." Finally we learned to share, to love, to cry, and to laugh together.

As a mature adult, I learned my father was a man of enormous strength and courage. Not the kind of power that moves mountains, for he was not a large man, but a man of quiet strength who had found a peace within himself and with his God.

So, who was this man we have come to remember?

We never really know another human being. Each of us has our own separate memories. But I can tell you that he was a spirit being, eternal, and endless, who followed a magnificent journey through this material world. Who went on a quest to learn to love more fully and to dissolve the illusions he had about his limitations. The love that he realized and gave to others while on earth will light the path through and beyond this world, beyond the show of earth to the place in spirit from where he came, the place from where all love and light radiates—the place we call home.

Let us rejoice, dance, and sing with our memories, for my father has finally gone home. Amen.

* * *

I only vaguely remember feeding one hundred fifty people at the clubhouse and being a taxi driver for people who had to park farther away from the clubhouse than they could walk. The same caterer, the one the residents of the mobile home park preferred, cooked and served the food. Mother's organ, prominently displayed on center stage, sang for the last time for Dad and his family. Roses from Dad's garden decorated the center of each table. Miraculously, every rose bush in his back yard was again heavily laden with beautiful, fragrant blooms. The more I cut, the more appeared.

Later in the afternoon, friends and relatives moved the celebration to Dad's home. We drank wine and beer and occupied the few chairs that remained in the house. In the evening, Joe arranged a dinner at the Claremont Hotel for just the two of us, reserving a quiet corner table with a view of San Francisco. My husband sat in sympathetic silence as I talked on and on, ignoring the river of tears flowing down my face.

* * *

A hawk swoops into a grassy field behind me. Egrets walk gingerly and delicately along the rocks on the shore. I listen to the comforting sound of the buoy, the call of sea gulls, and watch an occasional pelican rest on a boulder.

Albany Hill is in the distance behind me. It used to be covered with green grass, shrubs, and trees. Now, only modern buildings are planted and grown there while crowds of automobiles roam in and around them. Our childhood home on Burlingame Avenue behind the hill, the drive to Capwell's, the Drive-In theater in El Cerrito—I can see where they once thrived—they're no longer there. An era gone as my parents are gone. The emptiness that remains is something with which I am not yet familiar.

But I know if I venture into that dark deep emptiness, I will eventually find ME. For it is now my time—my time to be reborn, to rediscover *who* I am. To continue to experience. And to love.

I am about to embark on a new journey. I say goodbye to what has been, my eyes brimming with tears. Goodbye to my father, I will miss him so. Goodbye to my childhood home. Goodbye to my old neighborhood, my city, my county, and my state. I'll come by this way again, but it will be in another time, for a different purpose. It is time to move on, to grow, to learn, to evolve—to be born again.

* * *

"We identify ourselves with our parents. That is why when we lose a parent, we are confused and unsettled, as if we were standing naked on an unfamiliar highway. We are at a crossroads, and we don't have a clue about which way to go. Our protection, our home, our sanctuary is gone, and we are forever changed." —James Van Praagh, *Healing Grief, Reclaiming Life After any Loss*

Deep, deep in that darkness of sorrow I AM. It will take courage to go there, but I know I won't be alone; I have never been alone. Out of all this loss and sorrow will come a new life. God works that way. Nature works that way. There is always the right, the left, the darkness and the light. We cannot be born until we know death. For out of the darkness comes light. Out of sadness will come joy.

"THAT'S JUST THE WAY LIFE IS..."

Afterword

I had surgery two days after I returned to Massachusetts to find once again the strange cells so worried about were benign.

Jason has developed and matured into a fine, strong, and delightful young man, someone I am very grateful to have in my life.

David has continued his path as an artist, and at this point is known the world over as MOMO.

#

Thank you

My very special thanks to Hospice out of Kaiser, Hayward, for their sensitivity, kindness, caring and love—my family and I are eternally grateful.

To my wonderful family and friends who never wavered in their support for me, thank you.

NOTE FROM THE AUTHOR

Dear reader:

I hope the discussion ideas that follow will help you prepare for some of the challenges you will face as a caregiver. I recommend you read the entire book before tackling these questions. Reading the entire book will help you see how events unfolded over time and give you a frame of reference to organize your insights as you work through this material.

For each topic, there are specific days listed where you can see these issues playing out.

After re-reading the events under a topic, write down your own experience or anticipated experience as a caregiver and what you might do to make it manageable for yourself, your loved one and/or your patient.

Ideally, you'll be part of a group so you can discuss your ideas together and share your strategies.

If you are facing this, as I did, as an individual—I encourage you to engage your immediate family members in this discussion. These are tough issues. If you can surface them ahead of time and talk about how they may affect you and what the family members can do to support each other if these issues occur—you'll all handle the journey more successfully.

My best wishes to you.

Leslie Compton

Discussion Questions:

1. *February 27th, March 13th, April 5th, April 7th, April 21st*

   I am grateful for her thorough explanations and her honesty.

   As always she is honest and up front with him.

   She treats him with the respect and dignity he deserves.

   She continues to bring all of us comfort with each visit.

   She always takes the times to talk and listen to him.

   "It has been such a pleasure and an honor to have known you."

2. *Fear & Panic: January, February 16th, February 18th, March 6th, March 12th, April 5th*

   Afraid of my reaction if my fears are realized.

   How will I be able to handle this new crisis?

   Want him dead - don't prolong this any longer.

   I can't seem to relax. How will the rest of the night turn out?

   I am feeling nervous about that damn urine bag.

   Are we going to have to make a decision about IV feedings?

   Bill is having a panic attack.

   A sense of panic hovers over me like a heavy black blanket.

3. **Denial and Avoidance:** *January, Sunday, February 20th, February 16th, March 3rd, March 18th, April 19th*

   This can't be happening, not to my Dad.
   Wanting to detach
   Running errands are much easier for me than holding vomit bowls.
   Don't want to deal with this man's situation.
   I'll just pretend I am there instead of here.
   I've got to get out of this place. I'll return in a couple of hours.

4. **Helplessness:** *January, March 3rd, March 18th, April 6th.*

   There seems so little I can do for him right now.
   How can I survive this ordeal?
   Feeling alone and totally unprepared
   How much more can we take?
   Oh, God, make it stop!
   I haven't a clue how to make him more comfortable.
   I can't stand the overwhelming feeling of helplessness.
   I thought I was prepared for this.

5. **Medical Staff Issues:** *Sunday, February 4th, February 18th, February 29th, March 1st, March 2nd, March 13th*

   Why doesn't someone tell me what is going on?
   Hospice, you? You'll get rid of that organization in no time.
   I spend the next ten minutes arguing with this crazy surgeon.
   Oh no, you have been misinformed. Your father is not going home.
   The ostomy nurse

A seriously ill man is required to go to radiology twice in one day?

If medication is not given, he might die from a heart attack.

6. **Inappropriate comments and behaviors:**
   Sunday, February 13th, March 13th, February 28th, April 8th, April 14th, April 24th

   Oh well, none of us know when our time is really up, Clarence.
   You'll beat this setback.
   Too many cards spew meaningless wishes.
   "I know just how you feel."
   Friends denying dad's illness
   He is now having a bloody discharge from his rectum.
   My condolences, but it was for the best.

7. **Patient anger: February 14th, February 25th, March 13th, April 2nd, April 12th**

   Dad burst out with anger.
   My God. You didn't shop at Food-for-Less!
   Where were you last night?
   I have so much more to do and see.
   Where have you been all this time?
   His anger builds running over the brim of his already full cup.

8. **See-Saw of emotions: Sunday, February 22nd, March 8th, March 13th, March 15th, March 22nd, March 26th**

   I am not sure what is right anymore.
   I am on an emotional see-saw.

Where are the pretty ladies?

Please God, just have him close his eyes and not wake up.

I begin laughing uncontrollably.

I don't understand my conflicting feelings.

With a couple of more weeks like this, I'll get my energy back.

These ups and downs are terrible, never know what to expect.

9. *Guilt: February 4th, February 9th, February 25th, March 2nd, March 3rd, April 13th, April 21st*

I feel guilty because I harbor this anger.

How can I have thoughts like these?

Feelings of inadequacy about the care I have given him.

Listening to his story heavy guilt spreads through me.

I should be content catering to him.

How selfish of me to go out to dinner while he was so uncomfortable.

I am no longer able to endure. How guilty I feel.

10. *Stress - self care: Sunday, February 15th, February 22nd, March 1st, March 3rd, March 11th, March 13th, March 16th, April 8th*

Stress expresses itself in physical problems.

Everything requires so much effort. I don't have the energy I used to have.

I need to distance myself. I've safely locked away all of my emotions.

Shakes wrack my body.

The puzzle is a mindless activity. Time is momentarily suspended.

My bottled refuge is chilling.
My friend and I take a walk in the sunshine.
Bill and I sneak out before 8 o'clock.
Could I be having a heart attack?

11. *Caregiver's anger: January, February 4th, February 22nd, February 29th, March 2nd, March 18th, March 28th, April 5th, April 17th, April 20th, April 25th*

I resent this whole thing.
Why am I the one that has to put a complete hold on life?
Who is this person, some kind of sadist?
The hell with this mess. I hate this place!
What kind of an outfit is this?
This place has rules for everything; and damned be the person who tries to bend them?
Why doesn't he give it up?
I seethe with anger.
I am speechless!
The vultures are striking again!

12. *Jealousy: February 15th, March 18th, April 2nd, April 11th*

I don't see my Father light up anymore when I walk into
the room.
I am jealous of Sam.
Who is this Sam who can just walk into our lives and take over?
Damn it Sam. He is my father?

13. *Visitors: February 19th, March 10th*

> Grandson, Jason
> Two sisters who do not visit
> Elizabeth from Santa Barbara

14. *Letting Go: April 6th, April 23rd, April 25th, May 17th, Last Page*

> I will really miss that man.
> Kathy lets me yell and sob until I feel as though my body is crumbling.
> I can see what I have been feeling being played out over the toilet bowl.
> Everything is gone. Dad doesn't live here anymore.
> My Father has finally been able to go home.

www.ingramcontent.com/pod-product-compliance
Lightning Source LLC
Chambersburg PA
CBHW071308110526
44591CB00010B/825